Interior of Touro Synagogue (south-west view)

TO BIGOTRY NO SANCTION

Other works by Dr. Gutstein:

The Touro Family in Newport

The Story of the Jews of Newport

Aaron Lopez and Judah Touro

A Priceless Heritage

Articles on Judaica
  Universal Jewish Encyclopedia
  Collier's Encyclopedia
  American People's Encyclopedia

Editor
  Tercentenary editions of the Jewish Sentinel, Chicago
  Memorial Services for Day of Atonement and the Festivals

Contributing Editor
  Universal Jewish Encyclopedia Vol. 9

Co-Editor
  Jewish Family Bible

MORRIS A. GUTSTEIN

TO BIGOTRY NO SANCTION

A Jewish Shrine in America

1658-1958

.

. .

. . .

.

NEW YORK

BLOCH PUBLISHING COMPANY

5718 - 1958

Copyright, 1958, By

MORRIS A. GUTSTEIN

All rights reserved

Library of Congress Catalog Card Number: 58-14128
Printed in the United States

CONTENTS

ILLUSTRATIONS

FOREWORD

FEW PEOPLE in this world have been as history-conscious as the Jewish people. The Torah admonishes us:

> Remember the days of old,
> Consider the years of many generations.
> Ask thy father, and he will declare unto thee,
> Thine elders, and they will tell thee.

Jews have always recognized that they are what they are because of the spiritual and physical continuity of their peoplehood and the historic heritage bequeathed to them by the generations gone by. And the historic heritage in Israel has always been the accummulated spiritual and cultural treasures created by our people.

The writing of this book was stimulated by the historic heritage and spiritual values encompassed in the three hundredth anniversary of the Jewish community of Newport and by the designation of the synagogue, built by that community, as an American National Historic Shrine. Few are the Jewish congregations in our generation with such longevity, significance and fame. The Newport Jewish community has earned it because of its synagogue that has been preserved as a living symbol of the invincibility of the historic heritage and the concomitant spiritual values of Judaism.

The historic heritage of Judaism has been the blessing not only of Jewry but of all mankind. Particularly has it enriched

11

the American civilization which consists not only of mountains, valleys and prairies, factories and farms, highways, cities and hamlets, but of the hearts and minds of man, of faith and reason, art, letters and science and above all of the poetry of American living and the soul of American democracy.

In this book an attempt is made to relate some of the Jewish contributions to American civilization, so that we may draw from our American experience an appreciation of the principles of liberty and democracy and under freedom perpetuate a Jewish community rich in spiritual and cultural values to become the historic heritage for tomorrow.

The story in this book also calls upon the American Jew to rally to the support of the portals of the Jewish sanctuary— the synagogue. For it is evident that where a synagogue is built, preserved and maintained, there the Jewish historic heritage is not forgotten. This epic calls upon us therefore to rear a generation in America who will understand the value of living Jewishly, of carrying the banner of Judaism proudly, and of keeping the sanctities of our historic heritage in good repair, through knowledge and wisdom, religious observance, faith and piety, which have been rooted in the traditions of the synagogue.

The book also tells another story: the story of freedom and the dignity of man, the story of the spirit of Americanism. It tells that the Jew has come to America with a deep religious faith, which he kept alive and in harmony with different faiths. It reveals that having known poverty and privation in the Old World, he sought and appreciated the more, social justice and economic opportunity in the New World. Having experienced discrimination because of a different faith he could share the more in the moulding of the idea that every man has a right to be treated for what he is rather than for what his faith is or for what the color of his skin or eyes may be.

President Harry S. Truman, in writing to the synagogue in Newport when it celebrated its designation as a national site stated: "The setting apart of this historic shrine as a national monument is symbolic of our tradition of freedom which has inspired men and women of every creed, race and ancestry to contribute the highest gifts to the development of our national culture."

This therefore is a story that needs to be told.

The title of the book "To Bigotry No Sanction" is not without significance. The phrase has been taken from the address of George Washington to the *Hebrew Congregation in Newport.* It occured originally in a slightly varied form in the address of the Jews of Newport to our first president. This title has been chosen because, fundamentally, it constitutes the central theme of the story of this Jewish shrine in America. From the earliest pioneering days, the story of America and the Jew in America centered around either the striving for or the achievement of the ideal concept *to bigotry no sanction.* Certainly the pioneering Jewish communities in New York and in Newport in the seventeenth century, nay even in the eighteenth century were struggling to achieve this ideal. There were many occasions when attempts were made to sanction bigotry. However, the sturdy spirit of the colonists by the very nature of their diversified backgrounds and with the common denominator that drove them to these shores to wrest from the wilderness a haven of refuge and a place of opportunity to live and labor in freedom made necessary, for the common good of all, to forget narrow prejudices and to create a society, a culture and a civilization that gives no sanction to bigotry.

When the Department of Interior designated the *Touro Synagogue* in Newport as a *National Historic Site,* which made it the first and only national Jewish shrine in America, the United States reiterated and reaffirmed the ideal concept expressed by the Jews of Newport and repeated by George Washington, in 1790, that the government of this country gives to *bigotry no sanction and to persecution no assistance.*

The eloquent expressions of clergy and statesmen, and the voice of the people of all walks of life and of all religious, racial and cultural background, whose words were heard in and around this historic shrine from its dedication for worship, in 1763, and its dedication as a historic monument, one hundred and eighty-four years later, in 1947, re-echoed the refrain "To Bigotry No Sanction."

Nothing creative is accomplished by anyone without the assistance of others. I therefore want to record here for posterity my indebtedness to all who have been of inestimable assistance to me in my work and whose support and encouragement facilitated the publication of this volume.

My first gratitude is offered up to the Almighty.

I am indebted to the Officers, Executive Committee and Board of Directors of Congregation Shaare Tikvah for their continuous cooperation and their constant devotion to the work of the synagogue, which enables me to devote some time from my active ministry to study and research which made possible the writing of this book. Above all I want to record here my sincere gratitude and deepfelt appreciation to those whose generosity made the publication of this book a reality: Messrs, Herman Boxser, Sol Bolnick, I. B. Cohn, Bernard R. Cohen, Arthur Davis, Sidney De Love, Bernard Dunn, Leonard Fisher, Milton Feldmar, Sam Friedman, Raymond Kelner, Charles Lissner, Edward Lissner, Harry Lissner, Leo Michaels, Max Moschel, Isadore Shalowitz, Raymond Sher, Edward Sklarov, Seymour Smoller, Allen J. Stern and Sidney L. Weinberg.

I also wish to acknowledge my indebtedness to the many people whose works or words I quote.

In the preparation of a volume for publication much technical assistance and advice are necessary. I want to express my sincere appreciation to Max Applebaum and Maurice Zechman for the art work and the plates which make up the illustrations, to Leo

Block for designing and drawing the jacket for the book and to Rolo Fogarty for designing the title page. My grateful acknowledgement goes to the executive secretary of the Shaare Tikvah Congregation, Mrs. Max Denberg for her painstaking efforts in the preparation of the manuscript for publication. I want to express my thanks to Rabbi David Graubart, Rabbi Ephraim Prombaum, to my wife and our sons, Drs. Naphtali and Solomon and our daughter-in-law Judy, for reading parts of the manuscript and for making some very valuable suggestions.

It is my prayer that the people who will read this book will enjoy reading it as much as I enjoyed writing it, and they will come to the realization that in every aspect of our lives it is well to give to bigotry no sanction and to persecution no assistance.

Morris A. Gutstein

Elul, 5718, September, 1958

Chicago, Illinois

Tablet erected by U.S. Department of Interior designating the Touro Synagogue as a National Shrine.

Old Jewish Cemetery acquired by Jewish Community of Newport in 1677
(Courtesy Dr. B. C. Friedman)

TO BIGOTRY NO SANCTION

Chapter 1

HOW CAME THEY HERE?

O N a small street that less than two centuries ago was barren
land in the outskirts of a growing and striving city, in
Newport, Rhode Island, there stands a beautiful old synagogue.
No glamor or splendor of marble strikes the eye of him who
beholds this sanctuary. No display of riches and wealth invites
the attention of the passer-by. Yet, awe-inspired and aware of
a mighty past, stand those who tread the "lone floors where reverent feet once trod." With admiration and reverence one stands
in this holy place before the mystery of time and God, where the
present vanishes and the past flashes before the mind in beautiful
pictures, making an everlasting imprint on one's memory.

This synagogue is one hundred and ninety-five years old this
year, and is one of the four historic houses of worship in America
that have been designated by the *United States Department of
Interior* as national historic shrines.[1] The Jewish community that
built this synagogue is at least three hundred years old.

The evolution and history of the Jewish community of Newport, and the building of the famous historic synagogue, form a
most fascinating chapter in the history of the Jews in America,
and in the history of religious liberty in the United States.

This community and synagogue reflect the identification of
the Jew with American life for three centuries, since sturdy Jewish
pioneers threw in their lot with their fellow Americans in wrest-
ing from the wilderness a settlement of security and a haven for

19

those of all denominations and cultures seeking ampler living. In the relics of brick and stone of this historic shrine which the elements of nature left unharmed we can visualize many a pilgrim, pioneer and settler of Colonial days and many a hero of Revolutionary days.

The settlement of the Jews in Newport is associated with the search for religious freedom that the human soul has manifested since ages gone by and for which the New World was the first to offer a haven. This search for freedom goes back to the Pilgrims, among whom there was at least one Jewish family.

On September 6, 1620, a group of more than one hundred people - men, women and children - crowded into a vessel of 180 tons, now known as the famous *Mayflower,* to set out for the New World, where they could worship God according to their own conscience. Driven from England by religious intolerance, this small group of freedom-loving people looked toward the New World as a haven of refuge. After a turbulent journey on the high sea, nine weeks after leaving the European shores, on November 19, 1620, the weary passengers brought their vessel to anchor in the Cape Cod harbor.

They found here the opportunities for freedom.

These earliest pioneers are now known as the *Pilgrims.* But the name *Pilgrim* is not limited to the passengers of the *Mayflower.* The passengers of at least two other vessels, the *Fortune,* which arrived in 1621, and the *Ann,* which arrived in 1623, are also designated as *Pilgrims.* Among the passengers of the *Fortune* was one Moses Simonson, who was "from the Jewish settlement at Amsterdam." His daughter Rebecca married John Soule, son of George, who came on the *Mayflower.* Rebecca's son married Sarah Standish, who was a granddaughter of Myles Standish and also of John Alden. "The religious faith of the individual members of the colony," states the source of this information, "did not seem to enter into consideration" of the *Pilgrims* at the time. The settlement of the *Pilgrims* was thus the first manifestation of religious freedom in North America, in which the Jew shared.[2]

It was barely three decades after the Pilgrim Fathers landed on Plymouth Rock, that a group of other pilgrims, a group of Jewish refugees from the Inquisition, who were tossed by the raging billows and surging waves of the high seas for months, found a haven of refuge on the shores of the Atlantic, in the city of Newport. Here they were welcomed and received to share the "life, liberty and the pursuit of happiness" which are inalienable rights of every human being.

Newport was founded in 1639. Two years later the settlers defined their *Commonwealth* as a *Democracie*. The "Code of Lawes" adopted in that year specified that: "None bee accounted a delinquent for doctrine: provided; it bee not directly repugnant to yᵉ government or lawes established." The Code of Laws drawn up six years later, in 1647, concluded: "And otherwise than this, what is herein forbidden, all men may walk as their consciences persuade them, everyone in the name of his God, and let the saints of the Most High walk in this colony without molestation in the name of the Eternal their God, forever and ever." [3]

A few years later, Roger Williams, who founded Providence in 1636, declared: "I desire not the liberty to myself which I would not freely and impartially weigh out to all the consciences of the world beside." This pronouncement was followed in 1655 by his famous parable, which he addressed to "Loving friends and neighbors of Providence," in which he said:

> There goes many a ship to sea with many hundred souls in one ship, whose weal or woe is common, and is a true picture of a Commonwealth, as a human combination or society. It hath fallen out some times, that both papists and protestants, Jews and Turks, may be embarked in one ship; upon which supposal I affirm, that all the liberty of conscience that ever I pleaded for, turns upon these two hinges, that none of the papists, protestants, Jews or Turks be forced to come to the ship's prayer or worship, or compelled from their own particular prayers or worship, if they practice any. I further add . . . that, notwithstanding this liberty, the commander of the ship ought to command the ship's course, yea, and also command that justice, peace and sobriety be kept and practiced both among the seamen and all the passengers. [4]

Such sentiments could have no other effect than to invite to the shores of Rhode Island all those who, because of their religious convictions, could find no resting place elsewhere. Among these were the Jews.

The precise date of the settlement of the Jews in Newport cannot be definitely ascertained. Tradition, together with some documentary evidence have set 1658 as the year when fifteen Jewish families settled in Newport and became the nucleus of the Jewish community . This date has been perpetuated in all anniversary celebrations.[5]

A Glimpse of Freedom

The coming of the Jews to Newport is antedated by a century and a half of woeful history for the Jewish people in the New World. Soon after the first white man, Louis de Torres, a Jew forcibly converted by the Inquisition, and who accompanied Columbus on his first expedition, set foot on American soil, many of the exiles from Spain, and later from Portugal, sought refuge on the shores of the New World.

The Inquisition victimised the thousands of Jewish families who accepted baptism in order to save their lives but who secretly in face of all dangers preserved their love for Judaism, Jewish law and custom. Some had become true and faithful Catholics. They were all designated as Neo-Christians or Marranos, and dreaded the *Holy Office* and the fires of the *auto-da-fé*.

Suspicion of Judaizing led to imprisonment and torture or to what at times was a more fortunate fate, execution by burning alive or in the case of a penitent after strangulation.

The prisons of the Inquisition with their torture chambers, that can still be seen in some cities in Spain and Portugal, had small, dark, damp and dirty underground little rooms with stone walls and iron bars. The prisoner's food was dry bread and water.

Many Marranos, molested by the Inquisition, frightened and insecure, left the Iberian peninsula, seeking havens where they would not be troubled. Every little boat, fighting the waves of the Atlantic and braving the perils of the sea, carried some of the Marrano families, who maintained strict secrecy as to their origin. Some were lost at sea, some were sold as slaves, and some fell into the hands of pirates. Some did reach the shores of South America, hoping to live in peace. However, in vain was their attempt to secure peace. The clutches of the Inquisition extended across the wide ocean. Before long, the fires of the *auto-da-fé* were raging in the market places of the New World, with equal terror as in the old. Mexico, Peru, Central America and the West Indies, were the scenes of these dreadful acts in the religious drama that began more than four centuries ago.[6]

Not until the capture of Brazil by the Dutch, in the first half of the seventeenth century, did the Jews find in the New World a haven from persecution. Not much time was needed after the Dutch conquest of some of the settlements of Brazil, Bahia in 1624, Recife in 1631, and other settlements later, before we find in the New World large numbers of Spanish-Portuguese Jews forming flourishing and prosperous communities with synagogues, religious schools and spiritual leaders. Many of the members of these communities were former Marranos who now converted to Judaism openly.

It was not destined, however, that this remnant of Spanish-Portuguese Jewry should enjoy its happiness in the New World for a long period. After several attempts, in 1654, Portugal finally succeeded in subjugating Brazil to its rule again. In January of that year the Dutch yielded to the Portuguese: Recife, Mauritstad, Parayba, Itamarica, Seara and others of its possessions in America. With the conquest by the Portuguese came the destruction of the peace and happiness which the Jewish pioneers and settlers enjoyed in that part of the New World. With the conquest by the Portuguese came the end of a beautiful chapter of Israel in America, which lasted just about a quarter of a century.[7]

With the Portuguese conquest also came the Inquisition. The Dutch in their surrender insisted on the condition that the Jewish population be given the opportunity of leaving the country and escaping their new status of "relapsi." Over five thousand Jews

left Recife alone. Most of them returned to their native land
Holland, where they were received very cordially. A number
scattered through various other American colonies. One contingent,
consisting of twenty three people, after a perilous rescue from
pirates on high seas, sought shelter in New Amsterdam, now
New York, then a Dutch possession.

Strange as it seems, New Amsterdam, which at present
harbors the largest Jewish community in the world, was not ready
at that time to welcome these few poor and down-trodden sons
of Israel. The Calvinist clergy openly demanded that the Jewish
exiles from Brazil should be "sent away from here." Peter
Stuyvesant, the governor, wrote to the Dutch West India Company in Amsterdam:

> The Jews who arrived, would nearly all like to remain here, but
> learning that they were repugnant to the inferior magistrates . . .
> the deaconry also fearing that owing to their present indigence they
> might become a charge in the coming winter, for the benefit of this
> weak and newly developing place and the land in general, deemed
> it useful to require them in a friendly way to depart.[8]

In the meantime, until the answer arrived, granting the Jews
the right to stay in New Amsterdam with the same liberty as
their religious brethren were enjoying in Holland, the local
government issued a decree ordering: "that the Jews who came
last year from the West Indies and now from the Fatherland
must prepare to depart forthwith." This was not indeed a decree
of expulsion which required their leaving instantly; yet it was
sufficient to give impetus to some to seek a haven where they
would be received in more friendly fashion. This they found in
Newport, Rhode Island.

Newport thus harbored a few Jewish families, who fleeing
from Portuguese Inquisition in Brazil were not altogether welcomed in what is now New York.[9]

The settlement of the Jews in Newport may go back to a
date even earlier than the conquest of Brazil by the Portuguese
in 1654. About two decades ago a Dutch scholar published a
book of biographies and genealogies of old Jewish and Christian

families that figured prominently in the early history of Holland and its colonies as a free country.[10] Among the biographies there is found one about a Marrano family, headed by Habib Ben-Am, who originally came from Spain. The members of that family escaped from the raging Inquisition and lived at first for a short time in Amsterdam, Holland, where they openly confessed Judaism. In Amsterdam they were members of the community headed by the famous Manasseh Ben Israel who, aided and encouraged by Roger Williams, successfully pleaded for the admission of the Jews to England.

From Amsterdam the Ben-Am family together with others went to Brazil. Early in the fifties of the seventeenth century, it is said, Habib, his wife, two daughters and another small group, consisting in all of twelve people, came to Newport. They arrived in the winter. Though the Passover Festival was still a few months away they were concerned about the observance of the holiday. Their principal desire was to obtain *matzot* - unleavened bread - and a *Haggadah* - the service for the *Passover Seder*.

Habib Ben-Am had a brother Abraham Israeli living in Jerusalem. Some members of Habib's family were still living in Amsterdam, Holland.

Habib addressed a letter to Holland in the beginning of the winter, requesting the necessities for the observance of the Passover. In this letter, in harmony with the liberal spirit of Roger Williams, he said:

> This is the place for the Jews; here in the colonies of North America, especially in the colony of Rhode Island, it is expected that every inhabitant will be able to erect a Temple to his God. Our family will remain here. We are sure more Jews will gather here, as sure as we are that day follows night. And as we are determined to remain here we must think of the future. After the winter comes the Passover Feast, and so we must be thinking about that.

Habib asked that his relatives in Amsterdam request his brother in Jerusalem to provide him with *matzot*. When the *matzot* arrived in Amsterdam from Jerusalem, a relative of Habib

took charge of them, secured a *Haggadah* and proceeded to Newport. In the meantime a few other Jewish settlers - also former
Marranos - had come to Newport. All joined in the first celebration of the *Seder* in Newport.[11]

Shortly after this the Newport settlement was augmented by
a number of Jewish families who came from Barbados.[12] No
doubt they included also some of the Jews who escaped from
Brazil in 1654.

The first Jewish settlers in Newport are said to have brought
with them a *Sefer Torah* - Scroll of the Law - which they rescued
from the Inquisition. Having a sufficient number for the required
religious quorum, they are said to have organized the *Congregation Yeshuat Israel* - Salvation of Israel.[13]

At the time of the settlement of the Jews in Newport, the
residents of the city were divided into seven categories: 1) pro-
prietors - who were the original landlords with full rights;
2) freemen - who had all political rights; 3) inhabitants - who
were guaranteed protection but had no vote or office; 4) resident
aliens - who were simply given permission to live in the settlement; 5) bond-servants - who were there for debts; 6) slaves;
and 7) Indians. According to this distinction the Jews were *aliens*
or *strangers*. While they enjoyed full liberty and protection they
were apparently not free to trade like the other settlers.[14]

God's Acre

The first community act of the Jewish settlers was the acquisition of a burial ground. From one of the clauses in the deed of
the old Jewish cemetery, it is evident that the first Jewish settlers
left the town after their arrival, only to return a little later.
The restrictions in trading may have been the cause of their leaving. Their return was prompted no doubt by the charter obtained
in 1663 from King Charles II of England, which provided equal
protection to all residents in the colony regardless of creed.[15]

In the deed of the cemetery, dating from 1677, it is stipulated
that a fence be erected around the land, and "if it Should So Fall
out that yᵉ Jews Should all Depart the Island Again So as that

*Facsimile of the last part of the Deed of Purchase
of Old Jewish Cemetery in 1677*

there shall be none left to keep up & Maintain this Fence as aforesaid then the Said Land shall Return Again to the said Nathaniel Dickins." This stipulation would also suggest that the Jewish settlers had acquired this burial ground originally before 1677, and abandoned it when they left the settlement temporarily.

Because of the Jewish cemetery, the "Highway that Leads Down from ye Stone Mill toward Benjamin Griffins Land," upon

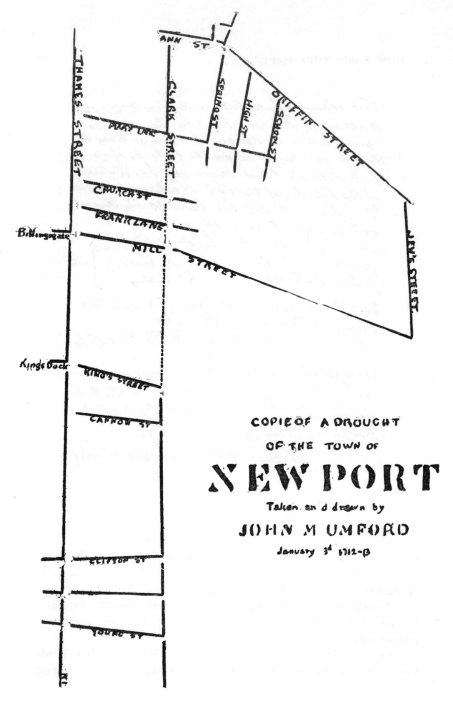

Map of Newport, showing "Jew's Street" (1712)

which it was located, came to be known as "Jew's Street." The street is so marked on a map of 1712. It is now part of the famous Bellevue Avenue.[16]

From the readable inscriptions on the monuments that are still extant in this historic cemetery, the earliest tombstone dates from 1761. Obviously the monuments of the burials from the time of the acquisition of the cemetery until that date have been destroyed. Some graves may have been left unmarked. In the course of erecting the fences around the cemetery in 1822 and in 1842, by Abraham and Judah Touro respectively, many old stones were broken and subsequently carefully heaped together and buried beneath the soil.[17] Thus many of the tombstones were lost to posterity.

Opportunities Under Freedom

The Jewish community in Newport grew slowly. As much as possible the people engaged in trade, local as well as inter-colonial and foreign. However, the peace of the Jewish community was interrupted by two events that turned out to be decisive and beneficial factors not only for the future of Jewish community life in Newport but for the entire city.

This happened in 1684 and 1685. The British Navigation Acts were in full swing.[18] Evasion of their laws stimulated the British to adopt more stringent ways and means to enforce them. Goods were confiscated, duties levied, and numerous other hardships were imposed by British agents on traders in the colonies. The Jew, having the additional disadvantage of being classified as an "alien" or "stranger," felt the blow first. In the eighties of the seventeenth century, Major William Dyre, Surveyor General of the colony, seized the estates of certain Jews living in Newport and brought their owners to trial.

The case, tried on March 31, 1685, attracted the attention of the outstanding members of the colony residing in Newport. Governor William Coddington, Deputy Governor Walter Clark, and other important persons, some of whom either before or after the trial occupied the position of governor, were present.[19]

Some nine months before the trial, another very important incident had occured. After the Jews were molested and some of their goods actually seized by warrant of the governor, they courageously presented to the General Assembly a petition for protection under the law. Simon Mendez and David Brown were the spokesmen. This occurred on June 24, 1684. The General Assembly acted on the petition the very same day. Without much hesitation and debate - for there was much important business to transact - the General Assembly:

> Voted in answer to the petition of Simon Mendez, David Brown, associates being Jews, presenting to this Assembly bearing date June 24, 1684, we declare, they may expect as good protection here as any strangers being not of our nation residing amongst us, in his Majesty's colony, ought to have, being obedient to his Majesty's laws.[20]

This resolution of the General Assembly certainly gave the Jews courage to defend themselves fearlessly. The defendants all appeared in court. "For want of a declaration in the office according to Law," the defendants were entitled to ask for a dismissal of the entire case, but they did not wish to do so. They were eager to hear a jury's verdict. And so the court proceeded:

> Whereas upon the information of Major William Dyre to our Honoed Governr against Mordecai Campanell, David, Daniell & Abraham Campanell, Saul Brown, Abraham Burges, Rachell the Widow and Relict of Symon Mendez Deceasd and Aron Verse Jews, Our said Governr granted a warrant to the Generall Serjat to sease the said Jews goods or estates answer the said informer his charge against them as aliens at this Court. And whereas he hath not brought the matter in such forme as our Law requires: Yett for weighty Reasons moveing, this Court doe see Cause with the defendants Consent that the Action shall Come to Tryall forthwith.

The verdict was not a surprise. The 'Jurrors' reported "Verdict, Wee find for the defendants and that the Plaintiff pay Cost of Court." The court ordered unanimously that "the distraint upon the defendants goods be taken off and their Estates so seized be Restored by the General Serjt." [21]

This decision not only assured the Jews the protection which had been given them by the General Assembly but actually gave them an impetus to trade and to engage in the larger mercantile pursuits. This attracted many new Jewish settlers to the shores of Newport and paved the way for the successful commercial era of the eighteenth century.

Towards the end of the seventeenth century, the Newport Jewish community was greatly increased by a large group of settlers who came from the West Indies, primarily from Curaçao.[22] These Jews, like their co-religionists already living in the city, were of Spanish-Portuguese origin. They became integrated with the rest of the community and lived in understanding and harmony with the city's population, which had a reputation of cultural refinement.

There is no record of the exact number of Jews who resided in Newport towards the end of the seventeenth or in the beginning of the eighteenth centuries. A few scattered references to Jews at the end of the seventeenth century came down to us in the municipal records. In 1688, at a Town Meeting, Abraham Campanal was granted a license for some purpose not specified. In 1700, one Daniel Campanal was fined 8 pounds and 15 shillings for misdemeanor. In the early part of the eighteenth century quite a large number of references to Jews have been preserved.[23]

In the latter part of the seventeenth century, some of the early Jewish settlers moved to New York. The first known *hazzan* - minister - of the New York Jewish community, the Reverend Saul Pardo, who in the Newport records appears as *Brown,* came from the Newport Jewish community. The first known *shammash* - sexton - of the New York congregation was Valentine Campanal, probably a member of the pioneering Campanal family of Newport.[24]

When Dean Berkley founded the "Philosophical Society for the Promotion of Knowledge and Virtue, by Free Conversation," in 1730, a chronicler records:

The Quaker, the Baptist and the firm supporter of the Church of England, maintained each his part; but the Quaker preacher and the

Jewish Rabbi, alike tenacious of their rules and doctrines, listened respectfully to the preaching of Berkley.[25]

The Philosophical Society was the intellectual fore-runner of the still-existing Redwood Library founded in 1747.

Among the first members of the library were: Abraham Hart, Moses Lopez and Jacob Rodrigues Rivera. Among the donors of money for the purchase of books were: James Rivera, Aaron Lopez, Isaac Hart, Abraham Hart and others. In the portion of the original collection of books preserved in the library today, there are a number of Hebrew texts, among them the philosophic book "Mateh Dan" by Haham David Nieto, which was the gift of Naphtaly Hart Myers.[26]

Early in the eighteenth century, Newport began to develop into the most flourishing mercantile city and leading ports in the colonies, rivaling New York in intercolonial and foreign trade.[27] The trading included slaves, which was found quite profitable. England encouraged the slave trade because it was a lucrative source of revenue. An import tax of three English pounds was charged for each slave. Primarily, however, Newport's commercial prosperity was the result of the import and export of all types of general merchandise from shoe-strings to carriages, and from the gradual industrial development in the city.

The Jewish merchants contributed greatly to the commercial and industrial development and consequent prosperity of eighteenth century Newport. They owned fully or in part boats that reached every port in the West Indies - Curaçao, Barbados, Surinam, Martinique and Jamaica - where prosperous and attractive markets were on hand. Jewish merchants were accused of monopolizing all of the West India shipping trade. Jewish-owned boats also reached Holland, the French colonies, the Spanish main, China and India. Early in the eighteenth century, a Mr. Levy obtained a patent for a 160 ton ship *Raft,* which could be loaded with over 1200 ton, built especially to export wood to England.[28]

Some of the boats owned by Jewish merchants were often captured by privateers, who brought them to Rhode Island for

Facsimile of original Court Record of
Trial of Jews of Newport in 1685

Jacob Rodrigues Rivera

Aaron Lopez

redemption. In 1723, the ship *Greyhound* owned in part by Jews was brought to Newport by privateers. In 1742, another ship *Three Brothers* owned by Benjamin La Mote and his three sons, Aaron, Abraham and Moses of Curaçao was likewise brought as a prize to Newport. Another boat owned by a Curaçao Jew, Joshua Henriques was brought to Newport by privateers five years later.

The Newport Jewish merchants, as a rule, took care of the captured boats and arranged for their release. When privateers brought the captured ship *Pearl* with two Jews, Emanuel Alvares Correa and Moses Cordoza, to Newport, Abraham Hart appeared in court and offered twice the value of the ship and its cargo, including court costs, in order to effect the release of his two co-religionists.[29]

Privateering was a profitable enterprise and was permitted by law as long as it involved only enemy ships. Some Jewish merchants built and sailed ships for privateering as well as for commercial purposes. In 1743, Moses Mendes and Abraham Pereira Musquita together with a non-Jewish partner fitted out as a privateer the ship *New Exchange* with twelve carriage guns, twelve swivel guns, and a crew of eighteen.

Three years later we find Abraham Hart fitting out his boat *Defiance* as a privateer with fourteen carriage guns, twenty-two swivel guns and a crew of one hundred and ten.

In 1747, the *Mary and Ann* owned by Moses Levy and two non-Jewish partners and the *King George* owned by Naphtaly Hart, were fitted out for privateering. A year later the *Rebecca* owned by Moses Lopez and two partners was fitted out as a privateer. Between 1758 and 1762 the records extant show that Naphtaly, Isaac and Abraham Hart fitted out as privateers the ships *General Webb, Defiance, Perfect Union, Dolphin, Confirmation, Diamond, Rising Sun, Lord Howe* and *Robert*. Moses Levy fitted out as a privateer the *General Well* in 1758.

The boats thus fitted out were also for protection against other privateering boats that might engage them in battle on high seas. [30]

Shipping in the eighteenth century was quite a hazardous, as well as a speculative, undertaking. Bad winds and weather, a storm at sea or a bad market often caused loss of money and could sometimes mean ruin and bankruptcy. Situations of this nature and critical business problems generally tend to create dissension among the people involed. When both parties were Jews often a Jewish arbiter would be called in to decide the controversy. In case of bankruptcy they appointed one or two Jewish go-betweens and fact-finders.[31]

The success of the Jewish merchants in Colonial Newport in the eighteenth century can be gauged from the fact that as early as 1742 the tax list included among its highest tax payers four Jewish merchants.

By the middle of the eighteenth century Newport developed also industrially to a great extent. An impetus to that development was given by the introduction of the sperm oil industry by Jacob Rodrigues Rivera, which extended its influence as far as New York and Philadelphia. The industrial boom and prosperity was to no small degree due to the Jewish residents of the city. For as active as they were in business so were they active in manu- facturing. As early as 1705, they had introduced the manufacture of soap into the colony. They joined in the established foundries as workers of brass and iron. They also worked as silversmiths. The year 1750 saw "The Scotch Snuff Manufactory, between Lopez Rivera and Cordoza in Comy." In 1753 the General Assembly granted a license to Moses Lopez for the manufacture of potash. In 1751 James Lucena introduced in the colony the manufacture of Castile soap.[32]

Between 1734 and 1763, one chronicler records that there were established in the colony of Rhode Island ten forges making iron ore into pig iron and hollow ware, six spermaceti factories, twelve potash works, three rope walks, one paper mill, besides other industries which included the manufacture of furniture and clocks.[33]

By 1775 there were in Newport twelve breweries, seventeen

spermaceti and candle factories, three sugar refineries, five rope walks, in addition to other industrial enterprises.[34]

In 1761, the *United Company of Spermacetti Chandlers* was organized as a natural outgrowth of the flourishing Newport industry. The Jewish interest in this association was predominant. It is interesting to note that the meetings of this association were postponed occasionally on account of the Jewish Sabbath, because the members of the Jewish faith would not attend.[35]

The Jewish residents in Newport were in constant contact with the merchants of other colonies, particularly with those in New York, who often helped each other financially. By the middle of the eighteenth century many Jewish residents of New York settled in Newport and joined in the intercolonial and foreign trade and in the industrial enterprises in the city.

Some of the Jewish residents in Newport became freemen. Moses Lopez was naturalized in 1750, James Lucena in 1751, Judah Franck in 1755. Other men, identified as Jews who were made freemen were Michael Philips, Joseph Silvester, and Joseph Jacob.[36]

Jewish citizens or freemen, had the same status as non-Jews. Jacob Myers was elected a grand juryman.[37] Among deputies from Newport to the General Assembly of Rhode Island and Providence Plantations in 1774 was Joseph Jacob.[38]

Some Jews of Newport built or bought houses and purchased real estate. In 1731 Naphtaly Hart purchased five lots of vacant land with 100 feet frontage, in the section called *East Point*. Moses Lopez bought some land and houses in 1749. Others followed, so that before long the greater part of *East Point* was owned by Jews.[39]

Jews took part in civic affairs, such as the enlargement of the jail, repair of the streets, and the arrangement of lotteries for these purposes. They joined the other fellow citizens in petitioning for reduced taxes.[40]

Commercial and Industrial occupations did not prevent Jews from serving in the armed forces of the colony and to participate in social activities. Zachariah Cohen is listed as a gunner on the

sloop *Queen of Hungary.* Jacob Judah served in the French and
Indian War in 1747. Michael Isaacs volunteered in the campaign
of 1755. Isaac Moses marched in the company of Captain J.
Whiting in 1757.[41]

In 1761 some of the leading Jews in town organized what
may be considered the first *Jewish Men's Club* in America.[42]
The Jews of Newport were very active in Masonry. King David's
Lodge, originally organized in New York and later removed
to Newport, was altogether of Jewish origin.[43]

Thus in Newport, the Jew and the non-Jew, though worshipping separately in different forms and languages, had the
same aspirations and met on equality in the street, in the home,
in the club or society, at the library, in the factory, on the vessels
and in the store, in the army and in the assembly throughout the
early part of the eighteenth century. This mutual friendship,
understanding and good relationship fostered at the time, were
fruitful later of many noble consequences.

Chapter 2

FREEDOM'S HOLY LIGHT

IT is difficult to realize that in the eighteenth century, the century of the American and French revolutions, the Inquisition was still in vogue in Spain and in Portugal, and many Marrano families in the Iberian peninsula were still living in dread of the *Holy Office* and the fires of the *auto-da-fé*. Two such families: the Riveras in Spain and the Lopezes in Portugal play an important part in the history of the Jewish community in Newport and in the building of the historic synagogue. The records tell us that in the middle of the eighteenth century, the fame of Newport attracted to its shores "many families of wealth and distinction," who fled from the Spanish-Portuguese Inquisition to Rhode Island freedom.[1] Among these families were the Riveras and the Lopezes. The Lopez and Rivera families were related in marriage abroad and continued to marry within the families in the New World.[2]

The Riveras flourished in Seville, Spain, for many centuries. They were Marranos, and subject to the dread of the Inquisition. At a very early date, some members of the Rivera family attempted to find a haven of refuge in Mexico, but in vain. As the clutches of the Inquisition reached over the ocean, we find that there too, in Mexico, they faced the same fate as their brethren in Spain. The fires of the *Holy Office* burned in the New World as well. Among the victims, between 1642 and

1645, were Dona Blanca de Rivera and Diego Lopez Rivera, who were accused of Judaizing.[3]

The first of this family to arrive in North America was Abraham Rodrigues Rivera, who came to New York in the early part of the eighteenth century. He was born in Spain and married there, and had lived there in full accord with the Catholic rites. Upon arrival in the New World, he underwent all the religious rites required by Jewish tradition, changing his name to Abraham, and his sons' names to Isaac and Jacob respectively, and his daughter's name to Rebecca. They were all born in Spain.[4]

Jacob Rodrigues Rivera, the son of Abraham, at first emigrated from New York to Curaçao, where he married and lived for a short while, returning later to New York. Here he was naturalized in 1746. Two years later he moved with his entire family to Newport where he introduced the manufacture of spermaceti candles, one of the most important sources of Newport's prosperity in the days that followed. Jacob identified himself prominently with the Jewish community of Newport. Next to Aaron Lopez he occupied the highest position in the commercial, social, and religious life of the growing and prospering Jewish community of Newport before the American Revolution.[5]

Aaron Lopez, the most outstanding Jewish merchant of Colonial Newport, who is referred to as the "Merchant Prince of New England," was likewise one of the Marranos who settled in Newport in the middle of the eighteenth century. He escaped from Lisbon, Portugal to find his freedom in America.

Aaron Lopez was born in 1731 into a family of Marranos, who for centuries through dread of the *Holy Office* had led a dual life. It may be of significance to note that only eight years before Aaron's birth, a renowned physician bearing the same name as Aaron, Doctor Duarte Lopez, probably a member of the same family, after whom Aaron was later named, was condemned by the Inquisition as an adherent to Judaism.

The father of Aaron Lopez was Dom Diego Jose Lopez, a man "much respected and esteemed in Portugal." Aaron, one of three children born to Diego from his first marriage, was baptized according to Catholic rites and christened Duarte. As far as one could observe Dom Diego was an observer of the rites of the Church and he gave his son Duarte as well as his other children, Jose, Michael, and Elizabeth from his first marriage, and Henry and Gabriel, from his second marriage, a religious upbringing in accordance with the doctrine of the Church. However, secretly, Dom Diego Lopez and his family observed and followed some of the laws and rites of Judaism in whatever manner possible. Within the family the father or mother continued the tradition of teaching the children to observe parts of the Jewish ritual in disguise, thus keeping them united at least in part with the religion of their fathers.

With all the rites of the Church, Duarte married Anna, a close relative, also a Marrano. This was the usual custom. The Marranos married mostly within their own group. Anna bore Duarte a daughter who was christened Catherine.

For a long time, some of the members of the family of Dom Diego Lopez, particularly his sons, were suspected of Judaising by the *Holy Office.* As a consequence Jose, the oldest son of Diego, escaped the country while his father was still alive. He was the first of the brothers to come to America through England, and to become known as Moses.[6] Another of Diego's sons escaped to Savannah la Mar, Jamaica, where he adopted the name of Abraham.

If one member of the family was suspected by the Inquisition all the rest were spied upon and watched carefully. Spies planted within the home followed the steps of every member of the household and reported back to the *Holy Office.* Duarte, too, must have been under close and scrupulous observation. No doubt he was correctly suspected of Judaizing, for upon the earliest opportunity he, his wife and daughter made their way to the New World, settling in Newport, where they found a haven of refuge from the persecution in Portugal. They were accompanied by Aaron's brother, Gabriel, who in his conversion to Judaism in the New World changed his name to David.

Henry, the other half-brother had died in Lisbon as a young boy.

In the New World, Duarte openly confessed Judaism by submitting to all necessary rites including circumcision.[7] Duarte and Anna were remarried with the traditional Jewish ceremony. His name was changed to Aaron, her name to Abigail, their daughter's name they changed to Sarah.[8]

A Father and Three Sons

The story of Michael Lopez, a younger brother of Aaron, is equally intriguing. Michael too was born in Lisbon and married a woman, Joanna, who bore him three sons, christened Edward, Joseph and John respectively.

The epic of Michael and his family in the New World begins in 1767. In that year Aaron Lopez lost his brother David. Upon the receipt of a letter of condolence from Isaac Da Costa on the passing of David, Aaron wrote to Da Costa:

> The Truly obliging Wishes your benevolence is pleased to pronounce for my Welfare are fresh proofs of the dignity of y'r Mind. May the Mighty hand retribute so generous Heart with multiplicity of Wordly Blessings and terminate all your undertakings perfectly happy.

Following this, Aaron Lopez adds a very significant and historic note, which points to the still ravaging Inquisition in Portugal, and reveals the conditions and fears of the Marranos in the eighteenth century:

> The same Powerful Being that deprived me of a good brother, has delivered from the reach of Barbarous Inquisition a younger Brother of mine than the Deceased, with his Wife and three sons; They arrived here the 11th July Last from Lisbon in a ship I ordered there for the better conveniency of their transportation: This piece of news I take the liberty to impart you, persuaded it will merit your applauze, both as a Judeo and a friend.[9]

It is obvious from this note that Michael and his family lived in dread of the *Holy Office* in Portugal. The opportunity to emigrate to America was considered indeed a deliverance from the Inquisition and persecution. Having found a haven in the

New World, Michael and his family, naturally, desired to convert to Judaism completely as did the other Marranos. Their conversion involved no little sacrifice. Because of the Inquisition, neither Michael nor his sons had been circumcised in their native land and this had to be performed while they were in the land of freedom.

On September 6, 1767, Aaron Lopez addressed a letter "per Post" to Abraham I Abrahams of New York, asking him to come to Rhode Island to circumcize his brother Michael and his three sons and bring them into the covenant of Abraham. The letter is a unique and interesting testimony of the situation and its contents is revealing:

> I have the singular pleasure of addressing you on the joyfull Occasion that presents me the arrival of a Brother of mine from Portugal with his Wife and three Sons; Their Errand being founded on the Grand Object of Glorifying the protector of Israel, are inspired with a Spark of our Old Father's Zeal & ready to obey the Divine precept.
>
> Therefore earnestly entreat your Devotion to Lead you to be the meretorious Instrument of their Obtaining the Covenant which happily Characterize us a peculiar Flock; I would have joined them before now, in anticipating this request, but the poor state of health my Brother has been in, made me think it prudent to wait his Recovery
>
> Should it suit Your conveniency to improve the first opportunity, after this reaches Y'r hands, it will particularly oblige one that sincerely professes to be
>
> Sir
>
> Your most Hble Ser't
Aaron Lopez [10]

Michael Lopez and his family at that time lived in Tiverton. Mr. Abrahams came to Tiverton, as per Aaron Lopez's invitation. On Tuesday, October 27, 1767, all four, Michael and his three sons, subjected themselves to the rite of circumcision. Michael adopted the name Abraham. Edward changed his name to Moses. Joseph and John adopted the names of Samuel and Jacob respectively. Michael was then fifty-six years old. Edward, Joseph and John were twenty-eight, twenty-four, and seventeen years old respectively. Michael's wife Joanna similarly underwent ritual conversion and adopted the name Abigail. In conformity with custom Abraham and Abigail married again in accordance with Jewish law and together with their children moved to Newport, where they joined the rest of the Jewish community and the synagogue and led a strictly Jewish traditional life.[11]

When Mr. Abrahams returned to New York, after a tiresome journey, he sent to Abraham Lopez and to others various ritual objects for their religious needs. In a letter addressed to Aaron Lopez, on November 20, 1767, Mr. Abrahams wrote:

> I arr'd safe here last fryday week after a very fatiguing passage having been at Fishers Island several days & at last came home by land from Huntington which was attended with no small expence however hopes all is for the better, I long to hear of your brother & family beg it by the earliest opp'ty.
>
> Here with send you double sett Tephilims for them being a present from Mr. Isaac Adolphus, he has no Tephilims to spare or would send some (sic). Also four setts for M'rs Lopes her sons with my compliments to her. I found my family all in health who join their best wishes to you & your wife.
>
> Your Most Hum'el Ser't
Abr'm I. Abrahams[12]

Aaron Lopez graciously replied to the letter:

> Your esteemed fav'r of the 20th ult. released us from the Anxiety we felt on the Event of your fatiguing passage & are exceeding glad you was at last restored in safety to your dear friends, whom have the pleasure to Learn you found in health.
>
> I delivered your kind message with the Tephilims to my brother Ab'm, who with his wife and children thanks you for your Friendly enquire after them and likewise to Mr. Adolphus for his Religious present, also dito my sister in law the Tephilims for the Boys, with your kind compliments.
>
> Please to receive in return an Ample & round Salutation from the Whole Family, who thanks to the Almighty is well. My brother & his family did not return from Tivertown till last Monday, they are all breavily and full of Devotion, God may increase it in them and in all our Brethren that we may cordially join to praise his mercifull regard for us that I am with particular esteem.
>
> Sir
> Your Most Hum'le Serv't
Aaron Lopez[13]

The Marranos who came to the New World, and here found a haven of freedom and the opportunity to live freely and practice the religion of their fathers still retained a certain fear lest they will be apprehended by the Inquisition. So deep was the impression of the necessity of secrecy in the observance of the Jewish religion that out of habit, some of the Marrano women, who came here to find freedom's holy light, as they walked the streets of Newport would tell their rosaries while they repeated their Hebrew prayers. This habit had been acquired in Spain and Portugal for the purpose of lending the appearance of Catholic form should they be surprised at their devotions.[14]

The Marrano families, who came to Newport quickened the religious life of the Jewish community. It was soon after their settlement in the city and joining the congregation that the movement began to build a synagogue.

Chapter 3

IN THE SERVICE OF GOD

SOMETIME before 1760, the Jewish community of Newport had engaged as its spiritual leader the Reverend Isaac Touro.

Many Jews have attained fame in various fields of endeavor in the pioneer days of the colonies and the United States of America. Of all, few are as well remembered as is the name Touro. Touro has become a by-word of the "noblesse" of Spanish-Portuguese Jewry in America.

The original provenance of the Touros was Spain, where they lived for a long time and where the family name was *Toro*.[1]

Persecution, inquisition and massacre dispersed the Toros of Spain from their native land. Through the Netherlands and the West Indies - havens of refuge for the expelled and down-trodden of Spain and Portugal - they found their way to North America. In the course of their wanderings the name became *Touro*.

The Touros produced a number of prominent men. It seems that for a long time the family centered about Amsterdam, in the Netherlands, where many of its members occupied important positions in Jewish community life. The records of the Sephardic community of Amsterdam contain frequent references to the name of Touro.

In 1664 one Abraham, the son of Judah Touro was *Gabai de Terra Santa* - chairman of the charities for the Holy Land - of the Spanish-Portuguese Jewish community of Amsterdam. Twenty

44

years later, in 1684, he was president of the congregation. In 1716, one of three sons of this Abraham, to whom the records refer as "Is," which undoubtedly stands for Isaac, was president of the congregation. Another son, Joseph, was administrator of the clothing for the poor scholars in the year 1702. In 1706, he was president of the society *Bikur Holim*, dedicated to the visiting and care of the sick. Joseph was also president of the *Talmud Torah* in 1711, and treasurer of the society *Bikur Holim* in 1732.

A third son of this Abraham Touro, Moseh, occupied the position of chairman of the charities for the Holy Land in 1707, and of president of the society for the visiting and care of the sick in 1710.

In 1683, towards the end of the seventeenth century, there flourished in Amsterdam, a great scholar and Bible exegete, whose name comes down in the records as "Juda Touro." In the beginning of the eighteenth century we find in the same city a distinguished philanthropist by the name of Manuel Touro. He expended money freely for all charitable purposes and may be the same as the Moseh Touro, the son of Abraham, who was both chairman of the Holy Land charities and president of the society for visiting the sick. That the same person should be known by two different names, one in Hebrew as recorded in the synagogue records and one used outside of the synagogue is nothing unusual.[2]

In the seventeenth century some of the members of the Touros began to emigrate to the New World, primarily to Brazil and the Dutch West Indies. A branch of the Touros lived in Brazil after some of the settlements were conquered by the Dutch, and very likely in 1654, when Brazil was retaken by the Portuguese, left for Amsterdam or settled in some of the West Indies.[3]

In the early history of Curaçao, there figures prominently one Eleiaho Hizkiaho Touro, who was gathered to his fathers in 1673, and is interred in the "Abode of Life" on that island. Clara de Ishak Touro was another early settler in Curaçao. She died in 1784. A Jahacob Touro married Rachel de Robles in

Curaçao. According to one authority, about ninety inhabitants departed that island in 1693 for Rhode Island, among them the family of Touro. Some of the Touros in Curaçao occupied prominent positions in Jewish community life. Ischac Touro was three times president of the *Talmud Torah*. Jehudah and Haim J. Touro occupied the same position. Jeoshuah Touro was a teacher.

After some of the colonists in Curaçao accumulated a little wealth they returned to Amsterdam and displayed splendid generosity as communal workers. The above mentioned philanthropist Manuel Touro was one of such early returnees from the island.[4]

In Surinam, we find members of the Touro family in the eighteenth century successfully engaged in "the promotion of commerce and welfare of the island," for which the Dutch government dispatched a contingent of Jews from Holland. In 1710, Aharon Touro left Amsterdam for Surinam. In 1736, Jacob de Eliau Touro lived in Surinam.[5]

Some members of the Touro family lived in Cayenne.[6] Some lived in Jamaica. A Moses Toiro, probably a corruption of Touro, fought heroically for the defense of Jamaica.[7]

The first of the Touros to achieve prominence in North America was the Reverend Isaac Touro. Whether Reverend Mr. Touro came directly to Newport from Holland or arrived from one of the Dutch colonies in the West Indies, cannot be ascertained with certainty. He is referred to in a contemporary record as a *hazzan* from Amsterdam, which may be taken as evidence that he came to North America directly from Amsterdam. Jamaica, Surinam, Cayenne, and Curaçao, in the West Indies, and Amsterdam, Holland, all share the honor of being considered at different times and by different authors the birth place of Isaac Touro.[8] As all cannot possibly be right, and as we find that in 1776, the Legislature of Rhode Island considered Touro a foreigner, the most logical conclusion would be that he came from Holland. However, Surinam and Curaçao might also have been the birthplace of Reverend Touro. These places were in Dutch possession, and a native from there would unmistakably be considered a foreigner in a North American English colony.

The reference to Isaac Touro as "a Chuzzan from Amsterdam," could refer to the fact that he was educated in Amsterdam, Holland. This would not be a peculiarity, for it was customary in those days, to send people from the West Indies to be educated in Holland, where academies of Jewish learning were flourishing.

Documentary evidence is not extant as to the exact date of the arrival of the Reverend Isaac Touro in Newport. In 1760, he officiated at a wedding in that city.

After Isaac Touro arrived in Newport, the spiritual life of the Jewish community was quickened. It was no doubt due to his coming that the Newport Jewish community began the erection of the beautiful house of worship, which was destined to become a shrine of American Jewry and a landmark in American history.

When Reverend Isaac Touro came to Newport he was in his early 20s and not married.

Among the Jewish settlers attracted to Newport before the American Revolution was the Hays family. The Hays family came to North America early in the eighteenth century, settling in and around New York City. They came from the Hague in the Netherlands where they resided for a period of time.

Of the six brothers who bore the Biblical names, Jacob, Judah, Isaac, Solomon, Abraham and David, Judah became naturalized in New York in 1729. In that year, he is recorded as a freeman in New York City. This gave him a better opportunity to engage extensively in successful commercial enterprises. He was one of the earlier Jewish merchants who owned his own vessels which were engaged in the profitable West Indies trade. One of his vessels was the famous privateer *The Duke of Cumberland,* a small craft of about 160 tons. During the French and Indian war *The Duke of Cumberland,* mounting sixteen guns and being manned by a crew of fifty, was used together with six other vessels, all owned by New York Jews, to prey upon enemy commerce.

Judah Hays was an active member and supporter of the *Congregation Shearith Israel* of New York, as can be seen from the records of the congregation. He was a generous contributor to all charitable causes and was by nature a very liberal-minded man.[9]

Newport's commercial progress induced him to settle in that city.

Of the children of Judah Hays the one who achieved most distinction was Moses Michael. Moses Michael, who was born in the New World in 1739, is best known as a leading figure among Jews in early *Masonry* in the United States. He was appointed Deputy Inspector General of Masonry for North America by Henry Andrew Francken, who had been commissioned by Stephen Morin of Paris, acting under the authority of Frederick II of Prussia, the Grand Master of Masons of Europe. Moses Michael Hays is prominently identified with the introduction into the United States of the "Ancient Accepted Scottish Rite" of *Masonry*. He received high distinctions in the Masonic Order being addressed as "The Most Illustrious Prince."[10]

Moses Michael Hays was a successful businessman in New York, Newport and later in Boston. He was one of the founders of the "Massachusetts Bank" and his name was the first to be entered on the bank ledger as a depositor. In his early days he was actively interested in the affairs of the *Congregation Shearith Israel* in New York in which he held the office of president. Like his father, he was a generous giver to all needy causes, a supporter of education and very much interested in civic affairs. His name appears on a list of benefactors of Harvard College and on the membership list of the Boston Marine Society.[11]

During the American Revolution the Hays family moved to Boston. The members of the family adhered strictly to the tenets of the Jewish tradition, at the same time they were extremely understanding of the religious principles of people of the non-Jewish faith. An eye witness made the following observation of the Hays in Boston.

> Both Uncle and Aunt Hays (for so I called them) were fond
> of children, particularly of me; and I was permitted to stay with
> them several days and even weeks together, and I can never forget,

Touro Street in Newport, showing the southern end of the Synagogue
(Courtesy Dr. B. C. Friedman)

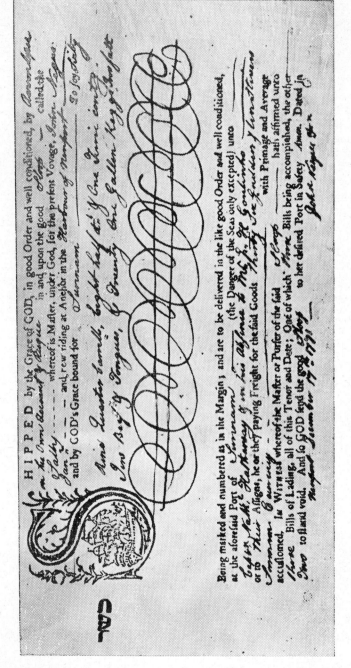

Facsimile of page from a Shipping Book of Aaron Lopez
showing the exporting of Kosher meats from Newport

not merely their kind, but conscientious care of me. I was a child
of Christian parents and they took special pains, that I should lose
nothing of my religious training so long as I was permitted to abide
with them. Every night I was required, on going to bed, to repeat
my Christian hymn and prayer with them, or else to an excellent
Christian servant who lived with them, many years. I witnessed their
religious exercises, their fastings and prayers, and was made to feel
that they worshipped the Unseen Almighty and All-merciful One.
Of course, I grew up without any prejudice against the Jews, or
any other religionists, because they did not believe as my father and
mother believed.[12]

On June 30, 1773, the Reverend Isaac Touro married Reyna
Hays, a daughter of Judah and a sister of Moses Michael Hays.
He was thirty-six years old and she thirty. Rabbi Isaac Karigal
of Hebron, in the Holy Land, who at the time visited Newport,
officiated at the marriage ceremony.[13]

Isaac and Reyna Touro were blessed with four children; three
sons, Abraham, Judah and Nathan, and one daughter, Rebecca.[14]

Fellowship in Faith

Reverend Isaac Touro was very popular in the community.
He was active in many organizations and was a member of the
Masonic Order. He was a fine singer and of extremely good
character. He was famous for his hospitality and his house was
open to all wayfarers. Among his friends he numbered many
non-Jews, the most noted of whom was Dr. Ezra Stiles, a Christian minister, later president of Yale University.

In an age when the fires of the Inquisition still burned, when
religious liberty was not acceptable to the average man, Isaac
Touro the rabbi and Ezra Stiles the Christian divine cultivated an
enduring friendship. They visited each other's homes, walked
together in the streets of the city, attended each other's religious
services, and discussed theological questions of mutual concern.
The only time Stiles ever dined with a Jew was in the house of
the Touros in the company of a visiting rabbi.[15]

Of the Hebrew scholarship of the Reverend Mr. Touro not
only the Jews of Newport profited, but to a large extent also

Dr. Stiles. After Stiles received the Doctor of Divinity degree
from Edinburgh in 1765, he felt the urge to acquire the Hebrew
language. Transliterated texts in the Redwood Library helped him
a little. Yet as late as May 1767, when Stiles was already forty
years old, he knew but ten of the Hebrew letters. It was then
that he solicited the aid of Touro. According to his first biographer
Abiel Holmes, Stiles,

> having walked a few times on the Parade with the *Huzzan,* who
> gave him the true power of the letters and vowels, he began to
> spell and read the Psalter:
> The *Huzzan* wrote for him the alphabet, with the vowels;
> gave him the sounds, and heard him spell most of the first Psalm.
> He also gave him the Rabbinical letters.
> In the five first days he read the 19th Psalm. Encouraged by
> his success, he soon found himself able to read about ten pages
> every morning after breakfast.[16]

Thus it was that two ministers in the service of God,
Touro a spiritual leader of the Jewish community worshipping
in the synagogue, and Stiles, a spiritual leader of a Christian
congregation worshipping in the church, walked the path of
life together; both amiably and cooperatively in the spirit of
brotherhood and in religious faith trying to make a better world.

Chapter 4

A COLONIAL SANCTUARY

THE bond which has held Israel together and insured its survival in spite of the many destructive forces, the fire, famine, sword, and dungeon, the rock and gibbet, and every human machination of torture, has been its spiritual heritage. The most potent symbol of this heritage has been the synagogue.

The abiding force of the Jewish people has been rooted in the synagogue, the institution created by Judaism for the education of the people in the principles and practices of its religion. The synagogue manifested to Jewry its unitary character. The synagogue has ever been the symbol of loyalty to God, Judaism and Jewry as well as the symbol of the Jewish will to survive as a people. Latent in the synagogue are the spiritual ties which bind the community of Jewry into a religious fellowship and brotherhood. Truly has it been said:

> Where there has been no synagogue to serve the wandering Jew as the rallying focus of his individual Jewish spirit and the physical nucleus of community life, centrifugal forces have rapidly swept him into the maelstrom of the gentile world. But where a synagogue has been established, thither Jews have come together centripetally from far and wide at stated intervals to reaffirm their basic unity, a unity of faith, religious life and tradition, a reflex of the unity of their God.[1]

"Let Them Make Me a Sanctuary"

In the eighteenth century all of Jewish community life centered around the synagogue. In the true historic tradition the synagogue was the house of prayer, the devotional center of the people in the community; the house of study, the educational center for young and old who sought guidance in the way of life as Jews; and the house of assembly, the community center, the rallying point of Jewish communal functions and social life.

It is little wonder, therefore, that the Jews of Newport, including the erstwhile Marranos, who identified themselves completely with the existing Jewish community, were most anxious to erect a sanctuary where they might freely commune with the God of their fathers, and retain their bond with the community of Jewry and with the historic tradition of their faith and people. Their major concern, was not only to build a synagogue whereto they could repair on occasions of joy to offer gratitude, on occasions of sorrow to find spiritual uplift and strength, or in the burden of human problems to find guidance, but also to build a religious school for the instruction of the youth in the verities of the Jewish faith and in the knowledge of Judaism and its spiritual and cultural heritage.

Religious services since the inception of the community were held in private homes. Originally the services were held in the home of Mordecai Campanal. Later the services were held in temporary rented quarters in the "Point" district.[2] In the middle of the eighteenth century, the religious services were held in the upper story of a house belonging to Moses Lopez and Dr. Williams on Duke Street, corner of Washington Square, which was formerly known as Queen Street.[3]

It was not until the middle of the eighteenth century that a synagogue structure was to become a reality. The location for the synagogue was chosen and the plans for the synagogue structure were apparently made known to the city officials before the land was actually bought. For, though the deed of the land dates from the middle of 1759, a map of Newport of 1758 indicates the location of the contemplated synagogue, which coincides with the exact position in which it is situated now.[4]

On "the thirteenth day of June, in the Thirty Second Year of His Majesty's Reign, George the Second, King of Great Britain & c., Anno ye Domi: 1759," the deed of the land for the building of the synagogue was signed. The land was located on Griffin Street and belonged to Ebenezer Allen of Sandwich, Massachusetts. It was purchased by Messrs. Jacob Rodrigues Rivera, Moses Levy and Isaac Hart, acting as trustees on behalf of the congregation.[5]

The land is described in the records as:

> One Certain Small parcel or lot of land Situate Lying and Being in the Township of Newport aforesaid, containing per Estimation Ninety two feet in Front or Breadth and One hundred and six feet in Length or Depth the same Being Butted and Bounded as follows (viz) Southerly on a Street Called Griffin Street, Westerly on Land of Jacob Barney, Northerly on a Street remaining yet to be laid out and Easterly on Land now in the possession and improvement of Matthew Cozens, be the same more or less within the said Bounds.

The cost of the land was "One Thousand five hundred Pounds in Bills of credit of the Colony aforesaid (Old Tenor)" amounting to $187.50.[6]

An appeal for funds in the local community did not yield enough to start building. Not having sufficient funds, and eager to begin the construction of the sanctuary, the Newport congregation, in accordance with a precedent established in 1730 when the *Congregation Shearith Israel* in New York built its synagogue, decided to appeal for financial assistance to other existing congregations in America and abroad. Letters of appeal, as far as we know, were sent to the congregations in New York, Jamaica, Surinam, Curaçao, London and Amsterdam.[7] The letter addressed to the New York congregation, dated in March, 1759, has been preserved and points out vividly the reason for the appeal and the motivation for building the synagogue:

> Sincerely desirous to establish a regular Congregation in this Town we therefore have Lately purchased a suitable Lot of Land,

Facsimile of the signatures to the Letter sent by the Newport congregation to Shearith Israel in New York, in 1759, soliciting financial
assistance for the building of the historic synagogue.

whereupon we design to Build a Sinaguogue; & for furthering our said Intentions, we have Likewise by Subscription raised a small fund, wherewith to Begin, and carry on the Work and which in due Time, we hope to see fully compleated. At present finding our Abilities not equal to our wishes, for finishing the Work, in so short a Time as we desire, we have resolved to crave the Assistance of the several Congregations in America, and as the Feast of the Passover is near at Hand, a Time when there will be a greatest appearance of our Brethren at New York; we embrace this opportunity to acquaint you with our proceedings, and Intentions, relative thereto; Intreating you to communicate the same, to the Congregation, at New York, & to supplicate for us, their charitable assistance, towards carrying on this work; either by a Freewill Offering in the Sinagogue; or Subscription, or in any way which may be agreeable to you.

The Newport congregation then continued:

When we reflect on how much it is our Duty to Instruct children in the Path of Vertuous Religion; and how unhappy the portions must be, of the children and their Parents who are through necessity educated in a place where they must remain almost Totally uninstructed in our most Holy and Divine Law, our Rites and Ceremonies; and from which place, they may perhaps never have it in their power to depart; when we farther reflect on how much it is our Duty to assist the Distressed; and when we consider the extensive Usefulness of Charity like this for which we now supplicate assistance; we can entertain no Doubt of your Zeal, to promote this good work.[8]

The New York *Congregation Shearith Israel* was very generous and responded very promptly after an appeal to assist the Newport congregation was made in the synagogue:

Comformable to your desire a Nedaba was made in our Synagogue the Seventh day of Pesach when a contribution of £149:6d was offered towards building at New Port a place of worship to Almighty God. Your pious design was a sufficient inducement to promote the Success of your request, we heartily, wish our mite may enable you to go on with the Holy building and that you maybe a Religious & prosperous Congregation.

We must now desire you will send orders for the money.

We sincerely wish you success in all your Laudable undertak-

ings, and that our God may graciously enable his People to do
Mitsvoth . . .[9]

On May 28, 1759, the Newport congregation appreciatively
acknowledged the generosity of the New York congregation:

> It affords us great satisfaction to find your letter of the 3 Day
> of Iyar (May-June) that our design for Building a public place of
> Worship to God Almighty has not only met with approbation
> but hath likewise been Zealously supported by our Brethren at New
> York as appears by the generous Freewill offerings made for that
> purpose in your Synagogue on the 7th day of Pesach last—
>
> It is our Inclination & we are truly sensible it is our Duty to
> return the Congregation at New York our most sincere & public
> Thanks for this Instance of their Generous Benevolence towards us
> and we Intreat You Gentlemen to do this good office on our Behalf
> in such manner place & Time as shall seem to you most agreeable.
>
> Your Hearty Wishes for the prosperity of Our Congregation
> and your sincere wishes for our Success contribute greatly to Incite
> in us an Ardent desire to compleat the Work which we have now
> undertaken —
>
> We Intreat you to remit the Monies which you have Collected
> for this Use to the Care of Messrs. Jacob Rods. Rivera Moses Levy
> & Isaac Hart in Gold either in Moidors or Johannes's. Moidors will
> be most advantageous.
>
> We Devoutly join with you in Prayer 'That Our God may
> Graciously enable his People to do Mitsvoth and are with Unfeigned
> Thanks to Yourselves & the Congregation at New York.[10]

The appeals addressed to the Jewish communities in Jamaica,
Curaçao, Surinam and London likewise met with favorable re-
sponses.[11] The generous assistance received from all helped in a
great measure to translate the ideal of the Newport community
into reality.

On August 1, 1759, the cornerstones of what is now the
oldest synagogue in America were laid. Aaron Lopez, Jacob
Rodrigues Rivera, Naphtaly Hart bar Moshe. Isaac Elizer, Isaac
bar Moshe, and Naphtaly bar Isaac Myers were honored with
laying the six cornerstones, to mark the corners of the synagogue
and its adjacent school-building.

Naphtaly Hart & Company acted as treasurer or financial
agents for the congregation during the construction of the syna-

gogue. They might also have been the contractors for the building.[12]

The building, begun with the laying of the cornerstones, continued at a slow pace. The days of "rush' were still in the future. It was not easy to get building material. The bricks had to be imported from abroad. The 196,715 bricks that were to be used for the structure were paid for on August 25, 1760.[13] The following year, the Newport congregation found itself again short of funds. On April 5, 1761, the Newport congregation through its president appealed again to *Congregation Shearith Israel* in New York:

> It is a matter of much Concern to the Congregation in this Town among whom I have the Honor to preside as Parnass for the Current year that they are Necessitated again to Supplicate the Charitable assistance of your Congregation who have already Chearfully & Generously Contributed towards finishing our Synagogue - Greatly disappointed in their Expectations from the Charity of other Congregations and the Cost of Building Rising to much more than it was Conceiv'd it would they now find themselves (unless in some way assisted by Other Congregations) unable to Compleat the Building - I do therefore by their Request intreat your good offices to Obtain the farther assistance of your Congregation towards compleating the same, either by a free will offering to be made in your Synagogue which to them Seems the most unexceptionable way or in any other method wch you shall judge the most agreeable to Obtain the good purposes Intended - the Congregation here Confidantly Relying on your Good Endeavours and the Zeal of your Congregation to promote so Charitable & useful an undertaking have no doubt but in due time I shall Receive your Favourable Answer hereunto—
>
> Wishing you and Each of your Congregation Length of Days with much Felicity, I have the Honor Gentlemen to Subscribe
>
> Your Obedient Servant
>
> Naph Hart[14]

More than a year later the Newport congregation appealed to some individuals in New York for furniture and other objects for the synagogue which was to take still more than a year to finish. Under the date of July 25, 1762, the president of the Newport congregation addressed Messrs. Joseph Simson and Samuel Judah of New York:

As we have now contracted with Workmen, who are actually at Work, to compleat the Hechal, Tebah & Benches of our Synagogue, are in great hopes same will be furnished by Rosasanah: We are getting ready such furniture & Utensils as are needfull, for which reason our Mahamad desires me to address this to you. Gentlemen, that you will be so kind as to make enquiry, who made any offerings of Furniture & Ornaments towards this pious undertaking, to receive & forward the same to us with convenient speed; that it may be here ready against the Time to Consecrating the holy Fabrick.

The gratefull sence (sic) we have of the Liberal assistance of your K.K. will put us in mind, of giving timely notice of the Dedication Day, that those Gentlemen who please to favor us with their Company may not be disappointed. Underneath I note what offerings came to our notice, if there be any more we leave to your enquiry, not doubting your Zeal in so Laudable cause.

You will always find in me a ready complyance to whatever Services I can render you, either in my publick or private capacity; wishing you health & prosperity I conclude respectfully

Gen—.

Your very hum. Servt.

Moses Lopez[15]

Appeals were also addressed to other individuals in other towns. These appeals did not go unheeded. Samuel Judah donated the *Ner Tamid* - perpetual lamp - and some candlesticks. The Tebah - Reading desk - came from Samuel Hart. Mr. Haym Meyers sent one hundred pounds of wax candles. Other contributions came forth from various other people.[16]

On December 2, 1763, after practically four years of building, the dedication of the new synagogue finally took place. Early in the afternoon the people began to gather in the synagogue, the men taking their places downstairs, the women seating themselves in the balcony. The invited audience consisted of Jews and non-Jews, including a great number of notables of the city and guests from other localities.

The ceremony of the consecration was calculated to bring out all the beauty of the synagogue and its service. At the appointed time, when the doors of the synagoue were closed and silence of expectation reigned within the walls of the holy edifice, three knocks were heard upon the closed door. The knocks came from without in accordance with the ancient ritual. After these three knocks, the voice of the Reverend Isaac Touro was heard, chanting in Hebrew: "Lift up your heads, O ye gates, and be ye lifted up, ye everlasting doors, that the King of Glory may come in." From within the synagogue came the response also in Hebrew: "Who is the King of Glory?" To which the voice of the Reverend Mr. Touro replied: "The Lord of Hosts, He is the King of Glory. *Selah.* Open for Me the gates of righteousness, I wish to enter them, I wish to praise the Lord." Whereupon a gentleman of the congregation designated for this honor opened the doors of the synagogue while at the same time another gentleman opened the doors of the Ark, and the Reverend Isaac Touro, followed by a number of gentlemen, entered the synagogue in procession. All these carried Scrolls of the Law covered with beautiful mantles, some of which were embroidered with gold. On the tops of the Scrolls were silver bells and ornaments, which provided additional lustre. As they advanced to the Reading-desk in the center of the synagogue, the congregation accompanied them with the chanting of selected portions from the Psalms.

All this time the entire congregation remained standing, intent upon the order of the procession. While the gentlemen carrying the Scrolls were standing near the Reading-desk, one of the leading members of the congregation lit the perpetual lamp, hanging before the Ark, and the Reverend Mr. Touro chanted the benediction in Hebrew, "Praised art Thou, Eternal our God, Ruler of the universe, who hast given us life and sustained us and enabled us to attain this season."

After this, seven circuits were made around the *Tebah* by different gentlemen, carrying the Scrolls of the Law, changing each time the circuit was completed. The circuits were made counterclockwise, beginning and ending at the Reading-desk. During the circuits the people chanted appropriate Psalms. When the processions with the Scrolls were over, the Reverend Mr. Touro recited a "Prayer for the Royal Family," after which the congregation chanted in Hebrew, "The Lord shall reign forever, thy God, O Zion, unto all generations, Hallelujah," and the final procession from the Reading-desk to the Ark took place to the chanting of Psalm twenty-nine.[17]

The consecration service made a deep impression on all present. When the *Newport Mercury* appeard three days later, it expressed the sentiments of those present in describing the ceremonies in the following words:

> In the Afternoon was the dedication of the new Synagogue in this Town. It began by a handsome procession in which was carried the Books of the Law, to be deposited in the Ark. Several Portions of Scripture, & of their Service with a Prayer for the Royal Family, were read and finely sung by the priests & People. There were present many Gentlemen & Ladies. The order and Decorum, the Harmony and Solemnity of the Musick, together with a handsome Assembly of People, in a Edifice the most perfect of the Temple kind perhaps in America, & splendidly illuminated, could not but raise in the Mind a faint Idea of the Majesty & Grandeur of the Ancient Jewish Worship mentioned in Scripture.
>
> Dr. Isaac de Abraham Touro performed the Service.[18]

Just as the Dedication Service made a profound impression upon the entire community so did the magnificent Colonial structure. It was the only house of worship constructed of brick and outstanding for its architectural beauty in the city.[19]

The synagogue as it stands today has not changed from its original appearance. It is a brick structure on a foundation of sandstone in a dugout shallow basement. The interior is painted white with a light blue ceiling. The exterior is in a buff color with the moldings or "belt course" and portico painted in a dark brown. The exterior was painted at a later date. The interior was painted at the time of dedication. Whether this was the original color scheme has not as yet been ascertained.[20] The interior is approximately thirty-two feet wide and forty-two feet long. The building stands at an acute angle with the street. Adjacent to the synagogue attached to the exterior of the north wall, is the schoolbuilding. It is a rectangular structure of two floors. In that building is the staircase leading to the balcony.

At the time of the dedication of the synagogue, Dr. Stiles was so impressed with the magnificence of the building that he described the interior of the synagogue in his diary in great detail. He also drew a rough sketch of a Holy Ark in his notes, showing the tablets of the Ten Commandments on top of the Ark. The enframement of the Decalogue and the carving or the wooden embellishments on the Ark doors are somewhat different than the ones in the Touro Synagogue.

In 1763, Dr. Stiles wrote:

> that the synagogue is now finished except the Porch & Capitals of the Pillars. The Front representation of the holy of holies, or its Partition Veil, consists only of wainscotted Breast Work on the East End, in the lower part of which four long Doors cover an upright Square Closet the depth of which is about a foot or the thickness of the Wall, & in this Apartment (vulgarly called the Ark) were deposited three Copies & Rolls of the Pentateuch, written on Vellum or rather tanned Calf Skin.

He then continued his description:

> A Gallery for the Women runs round the whole inside, except the East End, supported by Columns of Ionic order, over which are placed correspondent Columns of the Corinthian order supporting the Ceiling of the Roof. The Depth of the Corinthian Pedestal is the height of the Balustrade which runs round the Gallery. The Pulpit for Reading the Law is a raised pew with an extended front table; this placed about the center of the Synagogue or nearer the West End, being a Square embalustraded Comporting with the Length of the Indented Chancel before & at the Foot of the Ark.
>
> On the middle of the North Side & Affixed to the Wall is a raised Seat for the Parnas or Ruler & for the Elders; the Breast and Back interlaid with Chinese Mosaic Work. A wainscotted Seat runs around Side of the Synagogue below & another in the Gallery. There are no other Seats or pews.[21]

Above the Ark as it appears today there is a canvas oil-painting of the Ten Commandments, which, judging by the work and colors, and by the general execution, must have been painted by a skillful artist who followed instructions of someone who had some rabbinic knowledge. The tablets of the Commandments are surmounted by three crowns bearing the Hebrew abbreviations for *Crown of Priesthood, Crown of Royalty* and *Crown of Torah,* which are mentioned in the Mishnaic treaties *Ethics of the Fathers.*[22] No doubt these were painted to signify that these crowns must all have spiritual essence and foundations and must emanate from the Ten Commandments. The painting of the Ten Commandments is in a wooden frame with a triangular pediment and decorative carvings reflecting the classical revival in eighteenth century Colonial architecture, associated with the columns and the balustrades that run round the balcony. The Ark is an indispensable part of the entire architectural pattern of the interior of the synagogue. It is physically connected with all other architectural designs within the building.[23]

Since Stiles does not give the details of the painting of the Ten Commandments and its enframement above the Ark, and his drawing differs from the appearance of the doors and Decalogue enframement of today, it has been suggested that the present Ark is not the original one and that the painting of the Ten Commandments dates from the early part of the eighteenth century. These conclusions, however, are not acceptable in the absence of more corroborative proof and additional documentary evidence.[24]

We need add very little to the description of the synagogue by Stiles one hundred and ninety-five years ago, except to call attention to a few things that escaped the observation of the diarist or that were added shortly after the dedication. Thus Stiles did not note that the synagogue was not built at a right angle with the street, but at an acute angle. This was purposely designed, so that the Ark should be directly east. He did not note that the impressive Ionian columns supporting the balcony and the Corinthian columns extending to the ceiling number twelve, which is said to represent symbolically the twelve tribes of ancient Israel.[25]

Then there is to be added that shortly after the dedication five beautiful brass candelabra suspended from the domed ceiling adorned the interior of the synagogue. These candelabra were chosen to blend harmoniously with the *Perpetual Light* hanging in front of the Ark. Of the five candelabra: one of twelve branches is in the center; the other four, in the corners of the domed ceiling, are six-branched.[26] All are illuminated with candles to this day.

In front of the Ark there is a small platform, surrounded by a wooden railing. From this enclosure the sermon is preached, and the priestly benediction is pronounced.

The Reading-desk in the center of the synagogue, from which the prayers are chanted and the Torah is read in the old traditional melodies, is on a raised platform surrounded by a railing and is ascended by a few small steps on the north and south. Six brass candlesticks, two on each side of the Ark, and four on the corners of the Reading-desk enclosure were installed to blend with the hanging candelabra and the *Perpetual Light.*[27]

From the platform of the Reading-desk a few small stairs, apparently a secret passage to some hiding place, lead to the basement. It has been suggested that it once led to an exit into the street, which has since been covered and cannot be traced. This secret passage is said to have been a relic of the Marrano tradition of providing a hiding place in case of danger. This tradition was carried over into the land of freedom by the Marranos remembering the dread of the Inquisition and the spies of the *Holy Office,* who sometimes would apprehend their forbears during worship in the synagogue.[28]

From the time of the consecration until late in the nineteenth century there were no other permanent seats except those described by Stiles. Subsequently beautiful pews matching the entire interior were installed. Similarly, the illumination of the synagogue was improved first with gas and then with electric lighting. When the latter was installed care was exercised to have the fixtures resemble the still-used candle-light candelabra and candlesticks.

Extremely wide wooden boards were used for the floors, which remained uncovered from the time of the consecration until more that a century later, when they were covered with red carpets.

Two semicircular mahogany boxes were affixed to the columns in the west, each bearing the inscription "Charity Box." A clock that came from London, bearing the date 1769, was hung on the western side of the balcony.

In the adjacent school building, in addition to the stairs leading to the women's gallery, were located the sexton's quarters, and an oven to bake the unleaved bread - *matzot* - for Passover. The table for kneading the dough for the *matzot* it still preserved.

Covered wells in the synagogue yard may have been connected with a *Mikveh* - ritual pool - the location of which cannot be traced now.[29]

The Master Architect

Peter Harrison, who was an architect by hobby rather than by vocation and was called "the prince of the Colonial amateur architects," graciously accepted to design and draw the plans for the synagogue without any remuneration. For some reason, Dr. Stiles and the Newport Mercury did not deem it necessary to mention the architect's name. Perhaps this was because architecture at that time was not yet recognized as a profession, or perhaps it was because Harrison just drew the plans and the architectural supervision was left to the skilled house-carpenter Joseph Hammond, Jr. in accordance with the usual procedure in Colonial days.[30]

Since we do not have any minutes of the congregation's activities at the time and there are no records of any architectural fees, were it not for a Christian pastor it would not even have been known that Harrison was the architect of the Newport historic shrine. The Reverend Andrew Burnaby, a clergyman from Greenwich, England, in his travels in North America happened to pass through Newport during the construction of the synagogue. In recording his observation, Reverend Mr. Burnaby gives us some very interesting information concerning all places of worship in Newport in general:

> There are a few buildings in it worth notice. The court-house is indeed handsome and of brick; and there is a public library, built in the form of a Grecian temple by no means inelegant. It is of the Doric order, and has a portico in front with four pillars, sup-

Peter Harrison

Interior of Synagogue showing East wall and Ark

Exterior of Touro Synagogue

porting a pediment; but the whole is spoilt by two small wings, which are annexed to it. The foundation of a very pretty building is laid for the use of the free-masons, to serve also occasionally for an assembly-room; and there is to be erected a market house upon a very elegant design. The places of public worship, except the Jews' synagogue, are all of wood; and not one of them is worth looking at. They consist chiefly of a church, two presbyterian meeting-houses, one quakers ditto, three anabaptist ditto, one Moravian ditto, and the synagogue above-mentioned. This building was designed, as indeed were several of the others, by a Mr. Harrison, an ingenious English gentleman who lives here. It will be extremely elegant within when compleated but the outside is totally spoilt by a school, which the Jews insisted on having annexed to it for the education of their children.[31]

The biographer of the *First American Architect,* as Harrison is called, states that "Peter Harrison's career is a Colonial version of the American success story." He was born of a Quaker family, June 14, 1716, in England, later settled in America where he became an Episcopalean. He was trained "in the fear of God" and "brought up to a trade." He learned the mystery of ship-building and seafaring. Together with his brother Joseph, in 1739, he came to Newport, where he became the captain of a ship *Leathly* that sailed the high seas from the colonies to Europe and back with profitable cargoes. In 1746 he married Elizabeth Pelham. Early in 1747 he went to Boston to assume the command of a new vessel. After several adventurous voyages and enterprises, Harrison finally settled down to a successful business career in Newport. In 1761, he moved to New Haven where he passed away on April 30, 1775.

Peter Harrison learned and practiced design and architecture from various volumes in an intensive collection of books on the subjects which he accumulated. He had the largest and best architectural library in Colonial America. He began his designing career with the drawing of the maps of Cape Breton and of Newport in 1745. Three years later he designed the *Redwood Library* in Newport. This was the first building in America with a full temple portico. In his design of the Redwood Library, Harrison used engravings in Edward Hoppus' edition of *Andrea*

Palladio's Architecture published in London in 1735, which in turn was based on William Kent's designs which were found in Isaac Ware's *Designs of Inigo Jones.*[32]

In 1749, Harrison designed *King's Chapel* in Boston. This he based on James Gibbs' *Book of Architecture* and *Rules for Drawing.* Among the other Colonial buildings designed by Harrison are the *Freemason's Hall* and the *Brick Market* in Newport, *Christ Church* in Cambridge, Massachusetts, and *St. Michael's Church* in Charleston, S. C.[33]

Harrison's designs in architecture are considered "the most academic in the colonies before those of Jefferson." He had a natural talent for symetry and beauty and was wise enough to consult good sources.

Of all the buildings designed by Harrison, the Newport synagogue is the most beautiful, and is "one of the most perfect works of Colonial architecture." [34]

Professor Russell Hitchcock calls it "Harrison's Masterpiece," and describes it as a

> characteristic work of the international Academic reaction of the mid-eighteenth century in a rather unusual field, it would be of unique distinction in any country in the world.[35]

It has already been indicated that the general scheme of the interior is that of a two-storied hall with colonnaded aisles, Ionic below, Corinthian above. It has been described by architectural historians of note as the most impressive of classical edifices of the Colonial period. There is a harmonious unity in the architectural plan and design. Everything within the synagogue seems to belong there, and to be interrelated.

While there can be no doubt that Harrison, in accordance with his manner of work, used the literary sources of the architectural books in his possession as the guide for his designs and patterns, it must be admitted that he also used much of his latent talent, skill and imagination for esthetic effect. As to the Newport synagogue, the distinct form and pattern of its architecture reveal that he used in addition, established synagogue achitectural designs as they were executed in contemporary synagogues.

Four synagogues, two in America and two in Europe, had a direct or indirect inflluence on the architectural plan and design of the Newport synagogue. The two in America were: the *Shearith Israel* synagogue in New York, dedicated in 1730, and the *Mikvé Israel* synagogue in Willemstad, Curaçao, erected in 1732. The two in Europe were the *Sephardic* synagogue in Amsterdam, Holland, erected in 1675, and the *Shaar Hashamaim* synagogue in London, England, erected in 1701.[36]

The New York synagogue was about thirty-five feet square, twenty-one feet high, recessed from the street, and constructed in a manner that the Holy Ark was in the east "behind a railing of banisters." The synagogue was built of brick, had a ritual bath - *mikveh* - adjoining it, included a school house, and had a well and a pump on its premises. The interior was severely simple. The Reading-desk in the center was on a platform three steps above the floor, surrounded by a railing of banisters upon which were located the candlesticks. Suspended from the ceiling were five brass candelabra, four near the corners "holding sixteen candles" each, and one in the center "holding thirty-two candles." It had an elevated *banca* on the north, and a three sided balcony with a side entrance reached through stairs outside of the building.

The *Shearith Israel* synagogue of 1730, in New York "followed the general architectural pattern of its sister *Sephardic* synagogue in London and its mother synagogue in Amsterdam." [37]

The synagogue in Curaçao was constructed similarly. There too the balcony was reached by a staircase outside of the building.

Columns were found in all four synagogues. However, both the Amsterdam and the London synagogues each had twelve columns supporting the balcony and ceilings. The columns of the London synagogue were of the Ionian order and were arranged five on each lateral side - north and south - and two on the west side. In the Amsterdam synagogue there were six columns on each side - north and south - because the balcony extended only on the north and south walls.[38] In both, brass candelabra were suspended from the ceiling. Both the London and Amsterdam synagogues had windows rounded on top. The Amsterdam syna-

gogue was at an obtuse angle with the street, so that the Holy
Ark was located directly east.[39]

Among the Jewish residents in Newport and the leaders of
the congregation there were some who at one time or another
had seen all or at least one of these synagogues. Some coming
from Amsterdam might even have had engravings of the synagogue there. There were a number of published books in the
mid-eighteenth century which contained reproductions of the
Sephardic synagogue in Amsterdam.[40] It is quite possibile that
Harrison had access to some of these books. It is also possible
that in his travels Harrison himself had seen the London, the
Amsterdam and the New York synagogues.[41] Certainly the Jewish merchants of Newport who previously dwelt in New York
and were associated with *Congregation Shearith Israel* were well
acquainted with the New York synagogue.

Some of the Jewish residents had come originally from
Curaçao or had visited Curaçao in connection with their commercial enterprises. Certainly they must have had a clear picture
of the synagogue there.

It is probable, therefore, that Harrison was guided in the
architectural planning of the Newport synagogue either by personal observation of one or more of the synagogues mentioned
above, by an engraving of the Amsterdam synagogue, or by some
people who had personal knowledge of these synagogues.

The many similarities between the Newport synagogue and
the four synagogues described preclude simple coincidence. Even
if engravings of the Amsterdam synagogue were not available to
Harrison, or he did not personally see either the New York, the
London or the Amsterdam synagogues, the pattern of these
synagogues must have been pointed out to him by someone.
There is a striking resemblance between the essential elements
of the interior of these synagogues and those in Newport. There
is also a strong resemblance between the tablets of the Commandments, and the candelabra in these synagogues. Certainly the
same number of columns in the Amsterdam, London and Newport synagogues cannot possibly be accidental, since a lesser

number would have been sufficient for the Newport synagogue. Knowing that the Newport congregation was constantly short of funds, a few columns less would have helped to reduce the expenditures. Hence, the twelve columns in the Newport synagogue must have been copied from the London and Amsterdam synagogues for the symbolism of the tribes indicated before. It was good taste, more esthetic, and better classical revival not to have the columns of both tiers in the same order as in London. Harrison, therefore in accordance with published patterns in his library, made one tier Ionian and one tier Corinthian.[42]

Similarly, it must be said that the New York synagogue may well have been responsible for having a school building adjoin the Newport synagogue.

Harrison's ingenuity, however, was manifested in hiding the stairs leading to the balcony. Whereas in New York and Curaçao they were exposed, in Newport he managed to build them within the side building, creating a more esthetically pleasing structure.

The uniqueness in the architectural designs and patterns of the Newport synagogue points to the fact that Harrison must have used in addition to some guidance, his own ingenuity and imagination as well as architectural skill. His ideas were naturally influenced by the architectural works from his library and by the existing synagogues of the time. Thus he created "the most perfect of the Temple kind perhaps in America."

Some scholars have succeeded in tracing the original patterns followed by Harrison in designing the synagogue.

Professor Hitchcock maintans that on the Newport synagogue:

> Harrison lavished the resources of English Palladian design, copying the galleries from Jone's Whitehall banqueting hall, other details from Gibbs, and the Ark of the Covenant from Langley & Kent.[43]

Fiske Kimball, in his work *Colonial Amateurs and Their Models,* gives a very scholarly portrait of the architectural sources of the Newport synagogue, and traces all designs and patterns in the synagogue architecture to some work found in the library of Peter Harrison.[44]

It has been shown that Harrison used as a model for the interior the design of "John Webb's project for a chapel at Whitehall Palace in London," which was in his possession. This design called for an "arched two-story, galleried hall, having Corinthian columns superposed upon Ionic." [45] Various other details in the syangogue architecture have been traced to English academic pattern books, of which Harrison had a substantial number in his library.[46] In all instances, however, Harrison asserted his more classical taste and original ingenuity. This was particularly demonstrated when it came to the Ark, which in the Newport synagogue is altogether different from those in all four synagogues described above. The Arks in these synagogues were baroque. Harrison "eliminated all elements of the ornate baroque, wherever found in his models." [47] Appartently to Harrison a cupboard type of Ark with a "front resembling reredos of northern baroque church altars" as found in the London, Amsterdam and New York synagogues was old fashioned. He therefore designed the Ark for the Newport synagogue to be an "upright square closet" with four doors within the wall. He then added dignified panelling with the tablets of the Ten Commandments elegantly framed attached to the wall above the Ark, and an attic pediment on top of it. All this was much more in keeping with the classical revival that permeated the entire interior. It has been shown that for the Ark, Harrison followed similar designs he had used for the altar of King's chapel.[48]

For the enframement of the Decalogue, Harrison did follow somewhat the enframement of the tablets of the Commandments in the London and Amsterdam synagogues. In contrast to those synagogues where the enframement was treated as a baroque attic, in the Newport synagogue Harrison used instead an attic pediment, co-ordinating the mouldings of the Ark with the membering of the walls, thus integrating the Ark in the entire architectural design.[49]

It is to be noted that the balustrades around the balcony in the Newport synagogue are a little lower than they were in the other synagogues. It seems that here, Harrison was permitted to use his own discretion in order to conform with the general architectural pattern of the classical revival. These balustrades can also be traced back in pattern to Webbs' design of the Whitehall project.[50]

To complete the picture it should be added that the enframement of the doorway of the Newport synagogue resembles the entrance doorway of the Redwood Library, and the portico on the Ionian columns with intervening arches in a Palladian motif can be traced back to the same source as the portico of the Redwood Library. The hipped roof uniformly sloping on all four sides resembles the hipped roof of Kings' Chapel. The exterior two tiers of round-arch windows separated by a molding called a "belt course" are similar to the Old South Meeting House in Boston.

There remains only to explain the secret passage from the floor of the Reading-desk platform to the basement. It has been suggested that it might have been an emergency exit. Trap doors, secret staircases and chambers under cellars and between walls and floors were not uncommon in early American houses.[51] This would give so much more credence to the tradition that the erstwhile Marranos who built the Newport synagogue used this device to perpetuate a tradition inherited from the days of the Inquisition. For otherwise, why should they have provided this secret passage of escape in a synagogue?

From its inception, the Newport synagogue was admired by the community as a sanctuary blending dignity with beauty, richness with simplicity, and glory with sanctity. One who beholds this santuary is impressed not only with the historic associations of the edifice but with the magnificent balance in design, symetry of lines, and artistic harmony and unity. Truly one stands before this *Colonial Sanctuary* and, like Jacob when he awoke from his dream of angels walking up and down the ladder standing on the ground and reaching heaven, exclaims: "How full of awe is this

place! This is none other than the house of God, and this is the
gate of heaven." [52]

No one captured the spirit of this house of worship and the
impression of this shrine upon all who behold this beautiful
edifice, dedicated to the service of God, as did Emma Lazarus.
Upon visiting this historic synagogue in 1867, after it had been
closed for permanent worship well nigh three quarters of a
century, Emma Lazarus wrote:

IN THE JEWISH SYNAGOGUE IN NEWPORT

Here, where the noises of the busy town,
    The ocean's plunge and roar can enter not,
We stand and gaze around with tearful awe,
    And muse upon the consecrated spot.

No signs of life are here: the very prayers
    Inscribed around are in a language dead;
The light of the 'perpetual lamp' is spent
    That an undying radiance was to shed.

What prayers were in this temple offered up,
    Wrung from sad hearts, that knew no joy on earth,
By these lone exiles of a thousand years,
    From the fair sunrise land that gave them birth!

Now as we gaze, in this new world of light
    Upon this relic of the days of old,
The present vanishes, and tropic bloom
    And eastern towns and temples we behold.

Again we see the patriarch with his flocks,
    The purple seas, the hot blue sky o'erhead,
The slaves of Egypt, - omens, mysteries, -
    Dark fleeing hosts by flaming angels led.

A wondrous light upon a sky-kissed mount,
A man who reads the great God's written law,
'Midst blinding glory and effulgence rare
Unto a people prone with reverent awe.

The pride of luxury's barbaric pomp,
In the rich court of royal Solomon -
Alas! we wake: one scene alone remains -
The exiles by the streams of Babylon.

Our softened voices send us back again
But mournful echoes through the empty hall;
Our footsteps have a strange unnatural sound,
And with unwonted gentleness they fall.

The weary ones, the sad, the suffering,
All found their comfort in the holy place,
And children's gladness and men's gratitude
Took voice and mingled in the chant of praise.

The funeral and the marriage, now, alas!
We know not which is sadder to recall;
For youth and happiness have followed age,
And green grass lieth gently over all.

Nathless the sacred shrine is holy yet,
With its lone floors where reverent feet once trod
Take of your shoes, as by the burning bush,
Before the mystery of death and God.

Chapter 5

LIFE UNDER FREEDOM

BETWEEN the consecration of the synagogue in 1763, and the Declaration of Independence, many notable Jewish families were attracted to Newport and the community grew in large proportion. At one time it was estimated that there were over a thousand Jewish residents in the city. The growth was not only numerically, but also religiously and culturally. In 1775, when the New York Jewish community looked for a *shohet,* it inquired of "the Newport congregation if a suitable candidate for that office was available there." [1]

The majority of the Jewish population in the city were of Sephardic origin, but a considerable number taking an active interest in the affairs of the Jewish community were of Ashkenazic stock. The Ashkenazic element came principally from Germany, though it is to be noted that the Harts came from England, the Pollocks from Poland, while the Myers came from Austria and Hungary.

In affairs of the synagogue, the Sephardic element dominated because of their greater number and importance. The Ashkenazic members cooperated fully, so that harmony and accord existed at all times. The synagogue was deeded to Jacob Rodrigues Rivera the *Sephardi* and Isaac Hart the *Ashkenazi.* While Moses Lopez, a *Sephardi,* was President of the congregation one year, Naphtaly Hart, an *Ashkenazi,* occupied the position

74

another year. Beside the candelabrum of Aaron Lopez was hung that of Naphtaly Hart Myers, and beside those of Abraham Rodrigues Rivera, that of Jacob Pollock.

Centrality of the Synagogue

Jewish life in Newport was flourishing. The community, in all aspects, centered around the synagogue. The synagogue formed an indispensable part of the life of every individual Jew from his birth to his demise.[2]

The services in the synagogue were lengthy and in strict accord with the Portuguese custom of the Sephardic ritual. The Hebrew was spoken in the Sephardic pronunciation.[3] Services were held daily, mornings and evenings. They were well attended by young and old, and on the Sabbaths, Festivals and Holy Days, women constituted a large part of the congregation. Even when services were held in the dark hour before dawn, during the forty days of *Selichoth* before the Day of Atonement, worshippers were not wanting in the synagogue.

In the synagogue, the Reverend Isaac Touro was seated on the seat in front of the *Tebah* in the Center. Stiles tells us that Rabbi Karigal sat in the upper end in the East. The elders of the synagogue as well as the president were seated in the elevated enclosed *banca*. Visitors of high station that honored the synagogue with their presence were also seated in the *banca*. The men of the congregation either stood or sat on the south and north parts of the synagogue under the balcony, while the gallery running round the synagogue on the south, west and north was reserved for female worshippers.

The movements and motions during the services called out this interesting comment from a non-Jewish observer,

> How often have I stood just within the door, and seen the Israelites shuffling about with their hats on, and the Rabbi reading the Evening Service all being in motion, I suppose in imitation of the forty years' travel to Canaan.[4]

Preaching at the synagogue was not an integral part of the services and was only sporadic and mostly performed by visiting rabbis. Special prayers were offered on occasions for "all Nations, for the King and Royal Family and for the Magistrates of Rhode Island." Quite frequently non-Jewish dignitaries, such as the governor, judges and other state officials attended the services. Immediately after the services in the synagogue, the parents would bless their children by placing their hands on their children's heads.

The synagogue was supported by membership and voluntary contributions.

The congregation conducted an all-day school with an intensive and effective curriculum.[6] In addition to the religious studies, the children were given instruction in secular subjects, which included English, Dutch and Spanish.[7]

Man and his God

Eighteenth century Newport, as all Colonial America, was permeated by a religious spirit. Churches of all denominations flourished. By 1771 there were nine houses of worship, besides the synagogue in Newport. Theology was a subject of conversation. To keep debate on dogmatic religion out of the Philosophic Society, or to prevent discussion of synagogue affairs at the gatherings of the *Jewish Men's Club,* special provisions in the by-laws had to be made. When a cargo was shipped by boat from Newport, the customary shipping form read:

> Shipped by the Grace of GOD in good order and well conditioned by (............) in and upon the good (............) Called the (............) whereof is Master, under God, for the present Voyage, (...............) and now riding at anchor in the (Harbour of Newport) and by GOD'S Grace bound for (...............) And so GOD send the good (............) to her desired Port of Safety, Amen.[8]

Everyone walked with his God, and the Jews walked in the ways of their God.

The Jewish community was strictly traditional. The people were observant of their religious tenets. Jewish business houses and factories were closed on the Sabbath and holidays, and there are no records of boats owned by Jews that left the Newport harbor on Saturdays.[9]

The testimonies of contemporaries on this score are interesting
and enlightening. During the Revolution, when some of the
Newport Jews sought refuge in Massachusetts, one writer re-
marked:

> Though without a place of assemblying for worship here, they
> rigidly observed the rites and requirements of their own laws, keep-
> ing Saturday as holy time; but out of regard to the sentiments of
> the people among whom they were settled, carefully keeping their
> stores closed from Friday evening until Monday morning of each
> week.[10]

A little later, George Channing recorded a few interesting
items of like purport in his "Recollections of Newport." [11] In
speaking about Joseph Lopez, kinsman of Moses and Aaron
Lopez who was the chief clerk in the counting-house of Gibbs
and Channing, he remarks:

> He felt conscientiously bound to observe the 'times and seasons'
> peculiar to the Mosaic ritual. On Friday afternoons, he left the
> counting room about 3 P.M. in winter and at 5 in the summer, in
> order to prepare for the due observance of the sabbath on the morrow.
>
> Passover Week, and on the great day of Atonement, my friend
> would absent himself from business for two or three consecutive days.
>
> He was equally conscientious in making up to his employers
> for his absence on these holy days.[12]

Channing adds another recollection which is of interest and
worth quoting:

> Besides the family of Lopez (whose residence was on the north
> side of the Parade) I was acquainted with Mr. Moses Seixas, cashier
> of the Bank of Rhode Island, whose family occupied the bank
> building on the south side of the Parade. He and his son Benjamin
> who was the teller, were in stature short.[13]
>
> One set of the bank keys at the close of bank hours, was regularly
> left at our store for safe keeping by the teller. On the Jewish
> sabbath (Saturday), I was expected to take the keys to the bank
> when a Christian officer would be in attendance; for this service
> I always received some token, usually in the shape of Passover bread
> and bonbons resembling ears, in memory of those cropped from
> Haman, when hung for his intended cruelty to Mordecai.[14]

There are no records of conversions by Jews, but there are
references to a number of conversions of Christians to Judaism
in pre-Revolutionary Newport.[15]

Generally speaking, the Jewish families were large. Some
had as many as seventeen children.[16] The Jews did not live in
one particular section in town, though a great number of them
lived in what is called the "Point district." The houses in which
the Jews lived were in the majority of instances modest. A few,
however, were of large size. A British officer, during the occupa-
tion of Newport, calculated that he could station "200 men at
Lopez house on the East Side." [17]

In many instances the Jews had their business places or
factories adjoining or actually in their dwelling places. This was
a known practice of the Colonial merchants, whether Jewish or
Christian.

In appearance and apparel the Newport Jews were not different from the other people during the Colonial period. The
wealthier Jews wore aristocratic dress with the usual white wig,
as appears from some of the portraits that have come down to
us. Very few of the Jews grew beards. A German officer was
surprised to find the Jews of Newport, "not like ours known
by their beards and clothes, but dressed like other men, and
their women are in the same French style as the women of other
religions." [18]

From Dr. Ezra Stiles, who was very much interested in theology and mysticism, we learn about many interesting aspects of
Jewish life in Newport before the American Revolution. On
one occasion he informs us in his diary that the Jews of Newport
expected the Messiah almost daily. Under the date of August
10, 1769, he recorded:

> This day one of the Jews showed me a computation of one of the
> present Rabbins of Germany: wherein he makes "Time, Times, and
> a half" to denote the space from the last Destruction of the Temple
> to its Restorn and Return of XII Tribes. Times he calls 'Seventy
> Semitots' or 490 years, Times 980, half 245, total 1715, ending
> he says A.D. 1783, when Messias is expected.

Then he adds a very interesting note of a Jewish custom in Newport:

> The Jews are wont in Thunder Storms to set open all their Doors and Windows for the coming of the Messias.
> Last Hail Storm, 31 July, when Thunder, Rain and Hail were amazingly violent, the Jews in Newport threw open Doors, Windows and employed themselves in Singing and repeating Prayers, etc. for meeting Messias.[19]

Stiles was a frequent visitor at the synagogue. On one occasion he informs us about the introduction of the *Bar Mitzvah* celebration in Newport. Under the date of January 12, 1770 he tells us: "Went to the Synagogue this Evening and heard a Son of Mr. Lopez deceased, Aet. 13, read the Evening Service." Then he adds: "It is the Custom in the foreign Synagogue to initiate Boys Aet. 13, thus to read publicly. This is the first Instance in the Synagogue at Newport." [20]

Stiles also describes the *Pesah, Shabuot, Tishah B'Ab* and other services in the synagogue; the offerings and special prayers before the Ark, the chanting of the Torah and other interesting customs. At one of the services on *Shabuot,* Stiles tells us of a young boy of eight or nine, the son of Jacob Rodrigues Rivera, the erstwhile Marrano, who recited the *Maftir* - the closing portion of the Pentateuch reading - and *Haphtorah* - the Prophetic reading. He also tells us of another "little Jew Boy" who explained to the Christian minister the Scriptural meaning and ceremony of kissing the *tzitzit* - the corner fringes - on the *Tallit* - prayer shawl.[21]

The account of the services on Tishah B'Ab from the pen of Stiles is very intriguing:

> Went to the Synagogue, it being the Anniversary Fast for the Destruction of the Temple both by Nebuchadnezzar and Titus. They began VII and held till noon. The place of the ark was covered with a black curtain, and the lamp was put out. A table covered with black, stood before the *Tabauh,* and on a low bench sat the Parnass and *Huzzan.* The prayers were exceedingly melancholy, particularly when the *Huzzan* rose up, and went to the place of the holy of holies or the ark and mercy seat; where he wrapped

himself up in the black curtain, and slowly mourned out a most
solemn weeping and doleful lamentation, for the absence of the
Debir and *Shechinah*, for the cessation of the oracle, and for the
destruction of the holy of holies. The roll of the law was brought
out, without any ceremony covered in black and read at the foot
of the *Tabauh;* the portion was from Deuteronomy. Then the fourth
chapter of Jeremiah was read and three or four other chapters;
then the book of Lamentations; then the beginning and end of Job.[21a]

Before the American Revolution there were four other Jewish
congregations in the colonies, besides the one in Newport.[22]
Jewish emissaries from the Holy Land and from other parts of
the world frequently visited these pre-Revolutionary Jewish communities in order to solicit help either for a charitable institution
or for themselves. Among the most distinguished emissaries who
visited Newport for a lengthy period before the American Revolution was Rabbi Hayim Isaac Karigal. Rabbi Karigal, hailed
from Hebron in the Holy Land. During his stay in Newport,
it seems, he was considered the rabbi of the community. Karigal
and Stiles became great friends. They discussed "the Gemara;
the two Talmuds (of which he - Karigal - preferred the Babylonish); and the changes of the Hebrew language in different
ages." The frequent visits of Dr. Stiles to the synagogue were
reciprocated by Karigal with a visit to Stiles' church. The first
Jewish sermon published in America in 1773, was delivered by
Rabbi Karigal at the Newport synagogue, while Dr. Stiles was
in the congregation.

When Rabbi Karigal visited the church service, Dr. Stiles
preached on the text of Psalms, "Remember me, O Lord, when
Thou favourest Thy people; O think of me at Thy salvation;
That I may behold the prosperity of Thy chosen, That I may
rejoice in the gladness of Thy nation, That I may glory with
Thine inheritance".

The preacher elaborated this text as follows:

The Seed of Jacob are a chosen and favorite people of the most
High, and the subjects of the peculiar Care of Heaven, and of most
marvellous Dispensations. That not withstanding God's Chastise-
ments of their Iniquity & Imperfection in Calamities, Captivities and

Interior of Synagogue showing banca on North wall

Interior of Synagogue showing Reading-desk and north-east corner and wall (1872) (Courtesy, American Jewish Historical Society)

The Colonnaded Aisle in the south showing part of the wainscotted seats and column

The secret door and stairs leading from the Tebah to the basement of the synagogue (Referred to as the secret tunnel)

The School Building through which the stairs lead to the gallery of the Synagogue

Portico of the Synagogue

Torah Ornaments at Touro Synagogue

Table for kneading Matzot preserved in ante-room of the Synagogue

Rabbi Hayim Isaac Karigal

A

SERMON

PREACHED AT THE

SYNAGOGUE,

In NEWPORT *Rhode-Ifland*,

CALLED

" The SALVATION of ISRAEL :"

On the Day of PENTECOST,

Or FEAST of WEEKS,

The 6th day of the Month *Sivan*,
The year of the Creation, 5533 :
Or, *May* 28, 1773.

Being the ANNIVERSARY
Of giving the LAW at *Mount Sinai* :

BY THE VENERABLE HOCHAM,
THE LEARNED RABBI.

HAIJM ISAAC KARIGAL,

Of the City of HEBRON, near JERUSALEM,
In the HOLY LAND

NEWPORT, Rhode-Ifland : Printed and Sold by
S. SOUTHWICK, in Queen-Street, 1773.

*Title-page of sermon preached by Rabbi Karigal at
the Newport synagogue in 1773*

Dispersions; yet God hath not forgotten his Covenant with Abraham
and his posterity, but intends them great Happiness and will ful-
fill his promise in making them a very glorious Nation and a Blessing to the World in the latter Day Glory of the Messiahs Kingdom.
It should be the Desire of Christians and of all Nations, to partake
hereafter with Israel in their future glorious state, that we may share
& rejoyce in the Gladness of God's people & the Glory of his
Inheritance.[22a]

Other rabbinic dignitaries who visited the Newport synagogue before the Revolution, and of whose conversations and discussions with Stiles we learn from his diary, were: Rabbi Moses Malki of Safed, Israel; Rabbi Moses Bar David of Apta, Poland; Rabbi Tobiah ben Jehudah from a city near Cracow in Poland; Rabbi Bosquilla from Smyrna in the Levant; and a Rabbi Samuel Cohen, who came on behalf of the Jews in Hebron.

Of Rabbi Moses Bar David, Stiles tells us: "He is really a Rabbi. His title is: The Doctor, our Doctor, the great Rabbi, Moses the Son of David, an Ashcanazim of little Poland, of the holy Synagogue of Apta." [23]

It seems that these rabbinic dignitaries and emissaries were extremely welcomed in the city and highly respected. They were the guests of Reverend Isaac Touro. They were assisted financially and provided with transportation to the place they desired to visit after leaving Newport.

Before the American Revolution, Newport provided *Kosher* food for other communities. *Kosher* meat, certified by Reverend Isaac Touro was exported from Newport to the West Indies and other places. This continued also after the Revolutionary War was over. The shipping books of that period reveal shipments of "Jew Beef" to Barbados; "Casher Fatt," "Casher Tongues" and "Casher Cheeses" to Surinam; and beef and other meat products to Jamaica. A certificate testifying to the observance of the dietary laws of the meat products sent from Newport in 1787 has been preserved. It was signed within the precincts of the synagogue and was written originally in Spanish. It reads:

> I, the undersigned, certify that the 40 kegs of beef and two geeze pickled that are shipped by Mr. David Lopez on Board of the brigantine called Hannah, Captain William Howland, from this port for Surinam marked over the covers with the mark stamped *Kosher* M.B. and inside with four pieces of tape with the mark *Kosher* on each cover, are *Casser,* and that any Jew may without the least scruple eat of them, as they are prepared according to our holy law, and that is true I sign this with my hand in Newport, Rhode Island on the 23rd of Elul of the Year 5547 in the *Holy Congregation Yeshuat Israel.*[23a]

Matzot were baked in the community oven, and a communal *Seder* was held within the synagogue walls.

The Jewish community had a charity organization to help "the Poor of the Jewish Society in Newport," and the needy of other communities.[24]

Though living in a British colony, and using the English language as their vernacular, some of the Jews of Newport continued to use the Spanish and Portuguese languages. Some also spoke Dutch. There were already then a few from Poland who used Yiddish on occasions. Among the inscriptions on the tombstones are found many in Spanish and Portuguese besides Hebrew and English. In one instance - perhaps it is a remnant of a Marrano tradition - an inscription on a monument in the cemetery appears in Latin. Among the letters received by various members of the Jewish community in Newport before the American Revolution, there are some written in Yiddish.[25]

In such manner did these Jewish pioneers live under freedom in Newport before the American Revolution. They lived honorable lives and were highly respected for their integrity and resourcefulness. They lived not only for themselves but also for posterity. What they built, we inherited. The heritage we have received is now a Jewish shrine in America, and spells the immortality of those early Jewish pioneers of Colonial days, who, as many generations before them have prayed, and we in our day may continue to pray, in the words of Rabbi Karigal:[26]

> Oh most clement Creator, and Preserver of the Universe! May thine incomprehensible power inspire within us a desire of following thy right ways; and enable us to imitate the attribute of thy benevolence. Do thou, O Lord, enlighten the eyes of our understandings to comprehend some part of the mysteries contained in thy divine law; intirely (sic) dissolve the thick clouds of our ignorance and ingratitude; and permit that we may rightly come to the true knowledge of so precious a treasure, ever conforming our minds to thy divine will. Wilt thou, O most powerful God, grant us sufficient capacity to penetrate that great number of precepts, which by thy command we are under the obligation of observing; the whole being directed from thy benignity, for our full enjoyment both of temporal and

spiritual felicities. And lastly, wilt thou, O LORD, assist us with thine aid, so that in a continual observation of thy holy precepts, that happy and so long wished for time may draw near, when the disgraces of our nation shall forever be at an end; when thy divinity will again reside amongst us, and when the whole world will, as with one voice, say as we do - THE LORD will be KING over all the earth: In that day there shall be one LORD, & his name one. - May it be in our days.

                        A M E N

Chapter 6

TO BIGOTRY NO SANCTION

THE peace and serenity of Newport, and with it the city's economic prosperity and the flourishing Jewish community, were interrupted by what proved to be the decisive event in the history of the colonies - the American Revolution.

On the eve of the Revolution, the city boasted a population of eleven thousand amongst whom were some of the most educated and refined people in the country. From five to six hundred vessels traded from its port annually. Newport was a clearing house of all products consumed in the colonies; and in many foreign countries Newport products were indispensable.[1]

The Jews of Newport in a spirit of patriotism joined the Colonial cause. Moses Isaac, who later had the honor of entertaining George Washington in his home, Abraham Isaacs, Solomon Rophee, David Sarzedas, Seixas and others joined the fighting forces. Others contributed money, ammunition, boats and even cannons to the Revolutionary war. When the General Congress in Philadelphia ordered the Continental Fast Day throughout the colonies, the entire congregation gathered at the synagogue to join in prayer with the other colonists.[2]

At the outbreak of the Revolutionary war, the city of Newport suffered considerably. Its commercial, cultural and social activities were frustrated in view of the war entanglements. With the disintegration of the general community, the Jewish community naturally suffered. The population of the city began to diminish.

When Newport was occupied by the British, there remained just enough Jews to constitute a quorum for public services. The bulk of the Jewish community, in a spirit of patriotism for the Colonial cause, took up the "staves of wanderers" and left the city. The Reverend Isaac Touro, who had not become naturalized during his stay in Newport, and was therefore exempt from offering up a prayer on behalf of the British king, remained in Newport with the remnant of his congregation, continuing to conduct services at the synagogue. In accordance with tradition, he even allowed the synagogue to be used as a hospital by the British, this being the safest and most substantial building in town for such a purpose.[3]

By 1780, the Reverend Mr. Touro, resumed the traditional role of the Jew, by taking up his "wandering staff," and leaving Newport. Together with his wife and children, he removed to New York.

In New York, in the absence of the Reverend Gershom Mendes Seixas, who had gone to Philadelphia with the majority of the members of his congregation, the Reverend Isaac Touro for a while became the *hazzan* of the *Congregation Shearith Israel.* It was here that his son Nathan was born.[4]

The Reverend Mr. Touro did not stay in New York long. He left for Kingston, Jamaica, before the Reverend Mr. Seixas resumed his duties as minister. What caused his moving to Jamaica is unknown. Tradition has it that he sought a warmer climate in the West Indies because of his ill health. Shortly after his arrival in Jamaica, Reverend Mr. Touro at the age of forty-six breathed his last on January 8, 1784, and was interred in the "Abode of Life" in Kingston, Jamaica.[5]

After the demise of Reverend Isaac Touro, his consort Reyna and the children returned to the continent and went to live with her brother Moses Michael Hays in Boston. Her brother made the life of his widowed sister and orphaned nephews and niece very comfortable.

Unfortunately, it was not destined that Reyna Touro should enjoy the generosity of her brother for a long time. Nor was she to live to see her sons reach financial success and eminence. On the 28th of September 1787, she was "liberated for Paradise" at the young age of forty-four. Her remains were brought to Newport for interment, according to her last wish.

After the Revolution many Jews returned to town with the desire to revive the commerce of the city, but the community never regained the prominence it occupied in pre-Revolutionary days. Unfortunately Aaron Lopez, the most outstanding merchant and in whom all hope for revival was laid, met with an accidental death. Others gradually removed. The city in general lost it's importance in the economy of the country and declined completely commercially and industrially.

It was destined, however, that even in this period history should record a number of most significant events associated with the historic synagogue of Newport.

Between 1781 and 1784, the *Rhode Island General Assembly* met in the synagogue. During Washington's visit in 1781, a Town Meeting was held there to plan for his reception. During that period, too, the *Supreme Court of Rhode Island* held its sessions in the synagogue.[6]

A Visit by George Washington

The most climactic event associated with the Jews of Newport is the visit of George Washington to the city, on August 17, 1790. In the company of Moses Seixas and "the gentlemen of the party and the large number of gentlemen of Newport," the first president took a morning walk "around the town and the heights above it." Washington also took a walk in the afternoon. No doubt that it was during one of these walks that Moses Seixas accompanied the president to view the beautiful synagogue, which was the only building that retained its full splendor through the hard times of the evacuation. It is said the crowns on the tablets over the Ark caused the British to spare the synagogue.

When Washington was about to leave the city, Moses Seixas presented him with the now famous address on behalf of the

Hebrew Congregation of Newport, in which the Jews of America expressed the sentiment that the United States is "a Government which gives to bigotry no sanction, to persecution no assistance," a thought repeated by the Chief Executive in his reply.

The address to George Washington and his reply form the most outstanding expressions on religious liberty and equality in America.[7]

On behalf of the *Hebrew Congregation,* Moses Seixas addressed George Washington as follows:

To the President of the United States of America
Sir:

Permit the Children of the Stock of Abraham to approach you with the most cordial affection and esteem for your person & merits - And to join with our fellow Citizens in welcoming you to New Port.

With pleasure we reflect on those days - those days of difficulty & danger, when the God of Israel, who delivered David from the peril of the sword - shielded Your head in the day of battle: - And we rejoice to think, that the same Spirit who rested in the Bosom of the greatly beloved Daniel enabling him to preside over the Provinces of the Babylonish Empire, rests, and ever will rest upon you, enabling you to discharge the arduous duties of Chief Magistrate in these States.

Deprived as we heretofore have been of the invaluable rights of free Citizens, we now (with a dep sense of gratitude to the Almighty dispenser of all events) behold a Government erected by the Majesty of the People - a Government, which to bigotry gives no sanction, to persecution no assistance - but genirously (sic) affordens to All liberty of conscience, and immunities of Citizenship; - deeming every one, of whatever Nation, tongue, or language, equal parts of the great govermentel (sic) Machine: - This so ample and extensive Federal Union whose basis is Philanthropy, Mutual confidence and publik Virtue, we cannot but acknowledge to be the work of the Great God, who ruleth in the Armies of Heaven and among the Inhabitants of the Earth, doing whatsoever seemeth him good.

For all the Blessings of civil and religious liberty which we enjoy under an equal and benign Administration, we desire to send up our thanks to the Ancient of Days, the great preserver of Man - beseeching him, that the Angel who conducted our forefathers through the wilderness into the promised Land, may graciously conduct you through all the difficulties and dangers of this mortal life: - And

To the President of the United States of America

Sir

Permit the children of the Stock of Abraham to approach you with the most cordial affection and esteem for your person & merits — And to join with our fellow citizens in welcoming you to Newport

With pleasure we reflect on those days — those days of difficulty, & danger when the God of Israel, who delivered David from the peril of the sword, — shielded Your head in the day of battle: — And we rejoice to think, that the same Spirit, who rested in the Bosom of the greatly beloved Daniel enabling him to preside over the Provinces of the Babylonish Empire, rests and ever will rest upon you, enabling you to discharge the arduous duties of Chief Magistrate in these States.

Deprived as we heretofore have been of the invaluable rights of free Citizens, we now with a deep sense of gratitude to the Almighty disposer of all events behold a Government, erected by the Majesty of the People — a Government, which to bigotry gives no sanction, to persecution no assistance — but generously affording to All liberty of conscience, and immunities of Citizenship: — deeming every one, of whatever Nation, tongue, or language equal parts of the great governmental Machine: — This so ample and extensive Federal Union whose basis is Philanthropy, Mutual confidence and Public Virtue, we cannot but acknowledge to be the work of the Great God, who ruleth in the Armies of Heaven and among the Inhabitants of the Earth, doing whatsoever seemeth him good.

For all the Blessings of civil and religious liberty which we enjoy under an equal and benign administration, we desire to send up our thanks to the Antient of Days, the great preserver of men — beseeching him, that the Angel who conducted our forefathers through the wilderness into the promised land, may graciously conduct you through all the difficulties and dangers of this mortal life: — And, when like Joshua full of days and full of honour, you are gathered to your Fathers, may you be admitted into the Heavenly Paradise to partake of the water of life, and the tree of immortality.

Done and Signed by Order of the Hebrew Congregation in NewPort Rhode Island August 17th 1790

Moses Seixas, Warden

Facsimile of the Address presented personally to George Washington, on behalf of the "Hebrew Congregation in Newport," by Moses Seixas, Warden of the Newport synagogue, on August 17, 1790

when, like Joshua full of days, and full of honour, you are gathered
to your Fathers, may you be admitted into the Heavenly Paradise
to partake of the water of life, and the tree of immortality.

Done and Signed by Order of the Hebrew Congregation in New
Port, Rhode Island August 17th, 1790.

Moses Seixas, Warden.

The President replied:

To the Hebrew Congregation in Newport, Rhode Island.

Gentlemen:

While I receive, with much satisfaction, your Address replete with
expressions of affection and esteem, I rejoice in the opportunity of
assuring you, that I shall always retain a grateful remembrance of
the cordial welcome I experienced in my visit to Newport, from
all classes of Citizens.

The reflection on the days of difficulty and danger which are
past is rendered the more sweet from a consciousness that they are
succeeded by days of uncommon prosperity and security. If we have
wisdom to make the best use of the advantages with which we are
now favored, we cannot fail, under the just administration of a
good Government, to become a great and a happy people.

The Citizens of the United States of America have a right to
applaud themselves for having given to Mankind examples of an
enlarged and liberal policy: a policy worthy of imitation. All possess
alike liberty of conscience and immunities of citizenship. It is now
no more that toleration is spoken of as if it was by the indulgence
of one class of people, that another enjoyed the exercise of their
inherent natural rights. For happily the Government of the United
States, which gives to bigotry no sanction, to persecution no assistance,
requires only that they who live under its protection, should demean
themselves as good citizens, in giving it on all occasions their effectual support.

It would be inconsistent with the frankness of my character not
to avow that I am pleased with your favorable opinion of my
Administration, and fervent wishes for my felicity. May the Children
of the Stock of Abraham, who dwell in this land, continue to merit
and enjoy the good will of the other Inhabitants; while every one
shall sit in safety under his own Vine and Figtree, and there shall
be none to make him afraid. May the Father of all mercies scatter
light and not darkness in our paths, and make us all in our several
vocations useful here, and in his own due time and way everlastingly
happy.

G. Washington.[8]

To the Hebrew Congregation in Newport
Rhode Island.

Gentlemen.

While I receive, with much satisfaction
your Address replete with expressions of affection
and esteem; I rejoice in the opportunity of assuring
you, that I shall always retain a grateful remem:
brance of the cordial welcome I experienced in
my visit to Newport, from all classes of Citizens.

The reflection on the days of difficulty and
danger which are past is rendered the more sweet
from a consciousness that they are succeeded by days
of uncommon prosperity and security If we have
wisdom to make the best use of the advantages with
which we are now favored, we cannot fail, under the
just administration of a good Government, to become
a great and a happy people.

The Citizens of the United States of America
have a right to applaud themselves for having given
to mankind examples of an enlarged and liberal
policy: a policy worthy of imitation. All possess
alike liberty of conscience and immunities of
citizenship It is now no more that toleration is
spoken of as if it was by the indulgence of one
class of people, that another enjoyed the exercise
of their inherent natural rights For happily
the

the Government of the United States, which gives to
bigotry no sanction, to persecution no assistance,
requires only that they who live under its protection,
should demean themselves as good citizens, in giving
it on all occasions their effectual support.

It would be inconsistent with the frankness
of my character not to avow that I am pleased with
your favorable opinion of my administration, and
fervent wishes for my felicity. May the children of
the Stock of Abraham, who dwell in this land, continue
to merit and enjoy the good will of the other Inhabitants;
while every one shall sit in safety under his own
Vine and figtree, and there shall be none to make
him afraid May the father of all mercies scatter
light and not darkness in our paths, and make
us all in our several vocations useful here, and in his
own due time and way everlastingly happy.

G Washington

*Facsimile of the Address sent by George Washington to the "Hebrew
Congregation in Newport," in reply to the Address presented to him
by Moses Seixas*

Chapter 7

CLOSED ARE THE PORTALS

AFTER the visit of George Washington, the Jewish community continued to decline, so that by 1800, the "Jewish society" of Newport contained no one outside of the families of Rivera and Seixas and some of the relatives of the Lopez and Levy families.[1] The others had removed to various places in the United States. A great number went to New York, where they became members of the *Congregation Shearith Israel;* among these were the heirs to the title of the land on which the historic synagogue was built. Because of the lack of a required quorum - ten men - to hold public services, the synagogue was eventually closed.

On May 5, 1816, Stephen Gould, who volunteered to take care of the synagogue and the cemetery, wrote in his diary: "Widow Lopez and family, also Widow Rivera aged 96, sailed for New York." In October of the same year, he noted: "Moses and Jacob Lopez went to New York - This was probably a prospecting tour for the purpose of consultation as to the probabilities of bettering their condition." On March 18, 1822 Jacob Lopez died. On October 5, 1822, Gould wrote: "Moses Lopez, the last Jew, left Newport for New York."[2] This completed the dispersion of the Jews from their beloved city of Newport, which had welcomed them, giving them shelter and protection from hatred, bigotry and persecution.

The Scrolls of the Torah had been removed from Newport to New York earlier. An entry in the minutes of the *Congregation Shearith Israel* in 1818, reads:

> For a great number of years past there has not been services in the synagogue in Newport and the Seapharim have been deposited in the house of the late Mr. Moses Seixas of that place for more than twenty years and now under the charge of his Widow and son Mr. Benjamin Seixas.

Therefore *Shearith Israel* decided to request Benjamin Seixas, who by then was living in New York, to place the Scrolls of the Torah into the custody of the New York congregation upon the condition:

> If hereafter a Minyan shall be in Newport, R.I. and a request be made for a further loan of said Seapharim that the Trustees of the Congregation, will again loan the same for the purpose of being used in the Synagogue. And understanding that there are other Seapharim in the possession of Mrs. Seixas and Son, it is resolved that in case they will forward them to this City the Trustees will deposit them in the Eachal of the New Shool for Safe-keeping and return them when they shall be duly required so to do. And that this board will in their Corporate capacity indemnify Mrs. Seixas and Son for sending the Seapharim to this City to the care of the Parnass and will pay the expence of transportation.[3]

When the last of the Jewish families either passed into the *World of Eternity* or removed to New York, the title and the property of the Newport synagogue and cemetery legally passed into the ownership of the *Spanish-Portuguese Synagogue Shearith Israel* in New York.[4] It seems that the last representative of the Newport congregation formally handed over to the active *Congregation Shearith Israel* in New York the title of the closed synagogue, burial ground and other communal property.[5]

In the early '20s of the nineteenth century, the Newport synagogue was already considered the property of the trustees of the New York congregation. For in 1825, when the Rhode Island Legislature was considering repairing the building, they were prevented from doing so without consulting the New York congregation which was considered the rightful and legal owner of the property.[6]

With the closing of the synagogue, the building began to deteriorate. Channing in his "Recollections" observes:

> I well knew a Mr. Levara. During his residence in Newport, there was occasional worship in the Synagogue. Gradually these impressive services subsided, and finally died out; and then the building was left to the bats and moles, and to the occasional invasion, through its porches and windows, of boys who took great pleasure in examining the furniture scattered about.[7]

The physical condition of the synagogue property became the concern of the Newport city officials, and of Jew and non-Jew outside the city. In June, 1822, the Rhode Island American and General Advertiser wrote:[8]

> Sometime about the year 1690,[9] a number of Jews established themselves at Newport (R.I.) By industry and commercial enterprise they became wealthy, and their numbers increasing, they built themselves a Synagogue. When the late Rev. Dr. Stiles was Minister at Newport, he maintained a pleasant and friendly intercourse with the leading members of the Society, and spoke favourably of their character and religious temper. This Society, by removals and deaths, has of late years been fast dwindling away, and the last of the nation has at last taken his departure. Mr. Moses Lopez, the death of whose brother we lately noticed, was the only surviving Jew on the island. We understand that he has lately removed to New York, to enjoy the society of those of his nation who reside there.
>
> We are told that the Jewish Synagogue at Newport is still standing, and with a little expense might be long preserved, as a "handsome specimen of ancient architecture." It is expected that a number of the Jewish Society will assemble at Newport, and perform worship at the Synagogue during the summer, for the purpose of holding possession of the building.

During most of the nineteenth century when the portals of the synagogue were closed for public worship and regular services, they remained open for the public view, for the American Jew and non-Jew. The synagogue assumed a character as if it belonged to all America. It became a national institution and monument; a national shrine, not by resolution or proclamation but by its very nature, existence and historic background.

Noble Memories

Almost from the very inception there was a sacred and mysterious awe about this little house of God experienced equally by Jew and non-Jew. This awe was deepened and became even greater after the lack of a sufficient number of worshippers caused the discontinuance of the traditional daily, Sabbath and holiday services. The dispension of services seemed always temporary. There was ever an expectation of revival, an expectation that again the Psalms will be chanted in the ancient melodies, to speak from the hearts of man yearning for communion with God. The words of the poet: "Natheless the sacred shrine is holy yet" was more than poetry. It seemed to express the mood of the people who either beheld the beautiful historic synagogue on a visit or read or heard about it. Everyone, who saw the synagogue, felt as the poet continued: "Take off your shoes, as by the burning bush, before the mystery of death and God."

The Jews who left Newport cherished an unfading love for the city, and the people in Newport cherished a great respect for the synagogue and the Jewish cemetery, which to them were more than historic relics; they were symbols of joint striving for religious liberty, for the opportunity of freedom and the ideal of equality. These sentiments were, in a large measure responsible that this historic synagogue should not be destroyed by the elements or disappear in the course of time because of neglect, lack of worshippers and funds.

It was destined that this historic synagogue should remain a symbol of Jewish vitality in pre-Revolutionary and Revolutionary days, an emblem of the invincibility of Jewish faith and Judaism, and the will of the Jew to live. It was destined that this historic shrine should testify to the greatness of Americanism, to the spirit of true brotherhood and to the respect for the spiritual and cultural values of all people. So it was that a Christian family by the name

Abraham Touro

Judah Touro

of Gould, assisted by other non-Jews in the city, guarded, cared for, and maintained voluntarily the closed synagogue and the abandoned old Jewish cemetery, so that no vandal touch them, and their physical properties remain in tact.

The preservation of the synagogue and the cemetery, and their maintenance, was due, however, primarily to the beneficence of two gentlemen, Abraham and Judah Touro, the sons of the Reverend Isaac Touro.

Fortune had it that Abraham and Judah Touro both became wealthy in the beginning of the nineteenth century. Both were very charitable and generous. In their generosity and philanthropy they remembered the two shrines of the old Jewish community of Newport: the cemetery acquired in the seventeenth century, and the synagogue dedicated in the eighteenth century. Both left bequests for the repair and maintenance of the synagogue and cemetery. Judah Touro also bequeathed some money for a ministerial fund.

In his last testament, Abraham Touro willed:

I give Ten thousand dollars to the Legislature of the State of Rhode Island for the purpose of supporting the Jewish Synagogue in that State, in Special Trust to be appropriated to that object, in such manner as the said Legislature together with the Municipal authority of the Town of Newport may from time to time direct and appoint.[10]

The bequest was graciously accepted by the Legislature and Town Council.

The General Assembly established the "Abraham Touro Fund"[11] in 1823, for the purpose of keeping the synagogue and cemetery premises in complete repair.

Judah Touro willed:

I give and bequeath ten thousand dollars for the purpose of paying the salary of a Reader or Minister to officiate in the Jewish Synagogue of Newport, Rhode Island, and to endow the Ministry of the same, as well as to keep in repair and embellish the Jewish cemetery in Newport aforesaid; the said amount to be appropriated and paid, or invested for that purpose in such manner as my executors may determine concurrently with the corporation of Newport aforesaid if necessary.

The *City Council of Newport* graciously received the bequest
and established the "Judah Touro Ministerial Fund." [12]

Though the bequest for the synagogue by Abraham Touro
was accepted by the Legislature of the State of Rhode Island, and
the "Touro Jewish Synagogue Fund" was established as early
as 1823, nothing was done to repair the synagogue structure for
a few years.[13] The municipal authorities did not desire to
undertake any repair without the consent and possible guidance
of the legal owners of the structure, the trustees of the New
York synagogue.[14]

After consultation with the trustees of the *Congregation
Shearith Israel* of New York, and with their consent, an extensive
program of repair and maintenance was begun in 1827. Before
long the interior of the synagogue was redecorated, all necessary items repaired, the grounds and the exterior put in good
order, all in accord with the will of Abraham Touro and the
approval of the New York congregation. It was thus that the
historic building began to be preserved for posterity.[15]

From the original bequests, which were invested in bank
stocks and other securities, the capital of the Touro funds increased in large proportion. Whenever found necessary some
of the proceeds were used for the repair of the synagogue and
the upkeep of the old cemetery. If unused the proceeds were
added to the capital.

It was thus that these historic relics were preserved. The
generosity of the Touros made it possible for the new Jewish
families who arrived in Newport in the latter part of the
century to find an endowed and well kept-up synagogue for
regular public worship. This was a living testimony to a glorious and noble past, and a bright and hopeful future.

Because of the generosity of the Touros, the historic shrine
in Newport became known as the *Touro Synagogue.* When this
Colonial Sanctuary obtained that name can not be ascertained.
It seems that it was not done by resolution, but came about by
usage. In the second part of the nineteenth century the Newport
historic synagogue is referred to almost exclusively as the *Touro*

Synagogue in all the records extant. It was as if the people of America, instinctively expressed their gratitude for the beneficence of the two brothers Abraham and Judah Touro, through whose generosity, this historic American Jewish religious landmark was preserved for posterity.

Upon his visit to Newport, in 1858, the great American poet Longfellow recaptured the spirit and message of the synagogue and the cemetery and their preservation through the beneficence of the Touros, in his famous poem:

THE JEWISH CEMETERY IN NEWPORT

How strange it seems! These Hebrews in their graves.
   Close by the street of this fair seaport town,
Silent beside the never-silent waves,
      At rest in all this moving up and down!

The trees are white with dust, that o'er their sleep,
   Wave their broad curtains in the south-wind's breath,
While underneath these leafy tents they keep
      The long, mysterious Exodus of Death.

And these sepulchral stones, so old and brown,
   That pave with level flags their burial-place,
Seem like the tablets of the Law, thrown down
      And broken by Moses at the mountain's base.

The very names recorded here are strange,
   Of foreign accent, and of different climes;
Alvares and Rivera interchange
      With Abraham and Jacob of old times.

"Blessed be God! for he created Death!"
   The mourners said, "and Death is rest and peace";
Then added, in the certainty of faith,
      "And giveth Life that never more shall cease."

Closed are the portals of their Synagogue,
    No Psalms of David now the silence break,
No Rabbi reads the ancient Decalogue
    In the grand dialect the Prophets spake.

Gone are the living, but the dead remain,
    And not neglected; for a hand unseen,
Scattering its bounty, like a summer rain,
    Still keeps their graves and their remembrance green.

How came they here? What burst of Christian hate,
    What persecution, merciless and blind,
Drove o'er the sea - that desert desolate -
    These Ishmaels and Hagars of Mankind?

They lived in narrow streets and lanes obscure,
    Ghetto and Judenstrass, in mirk and mire;
Taught in the school of patience to endure
    The life of anguish and the death of fire.

All their lives long, with the unleaven bread,
    And bitter herbs or exile and its fears,
The wasting famine of the heart they fed,
    And slaked its thirst with marah of their tears.

Anathema maranatha! was the cry
    That rang from town to town, from street to street,
At every gate the accursed Mordecai
    Was mocked and jeered, and spurned by Christian feet.

Pride and humiliation hand in hand
    Walked with them through the world where'er they went;
Trampled and beaten were they as the sand,
    And yet unshaken as the continent.

For in the background figures vague and vast
Of patriarchs and prophets rose sublime,
And all the great traditions of the Past
They saw reflected in the coming time.

And thus forever with revered look
The mystic volume of the world they read,
Spelling it backward, like a Hebrew book,
Till life became a Legend of the Dead.

But ah! what once has been shall be no more!
The groaning earth in travail and in pain
Brings forth its races, but does not restore,
And the dead nations never rise again.

Well may we repeat the words of Longfellow concerning the *Touro Synagogue* and old cemetery in Newport during the middle of the nineteenth century.

Closed are the portals of their synagogue,
No Psalms of David now the silence break,
No Rabbi reads the ancient Decalogue
In the grand dialect the Prophets spake.

Gone are the living, but the dead remain
And not neglected; for a hand unseen,
Scattering its bounty, like a summer rain
Still keeps their graves and their remembrance green.

Chapter 8

THE SACRED SHRINE IS HOLY YET

THOUGH the *Colonial Sanctuary* was physically closed during most of the nineteenth century because of lack of a congregation, spiritually the synagogue remained open, for people always sought refuge in it in life and in death. Thus the synagogue was open on many occasions for funeral services of former members who passed away in other places and who willed that their remains be interred in the old Jewish cemetery in Newport; it welcomed visitors all the time; and it was used for occasional private and family services and prayers and at times for public services. As early as the '20s of the century, the synagogue was opened for public services during the summer.[1]

A few years ago Dr. David de Sola Pool, spiritual leader of the *Congregation Shearith Israel* of New York, discovered some old scrap-books on the historic synagogue in Newport.[2] On the first page of one of the books the following lengthy account is reported:

> This Sacred Edifice was reopened for Divine Service on Sabbath the 25th day of Ab 5610, corresponding with the 2/3 days of August 1850, after a suspension of about sixty years by a few of the children of Israel temporarily sojourning in this City, and thus continued during the warm season whilst the requisite number remained to form a Congregation.[3]
>
> In the absence of a professional Reader the Hebrew services on this occasion (commencing on Friday evening) were performed by several individuals, (including descendants of some of the old

Congregation of the 2, 3, and 4th generations) under the super-
intendance of the Revd. Morris S. Raphall, (late of Birmingham,
England) Lecturer and preacher to the Congregation B'nai Yeshurun,
New York, who delivered a Discourse in English, and read the
portion of the sacred law of Moses appropriate to the day.

The names of those present on this interesting occasion, and
subsequently during the season participating in the holy worship
conducted in accordance with the ritual of the Spanish and Portuguese Jews as had always prevailed in this Synagogue are hereto
subjoined-

The services on the first Sabbath were conducted by

Revd. M. S. Raphall
Theodore I. Seixas
Samuel Cohen   } of New York
Asher Kursheedt
Gustavus I. Isaacs

and those of the succeeding Sabbaths by Revd. Eleazar Lyons of
Boston, Asher Kursheedt, acting as Parnass (President) and Joshua
Isaacs as Secretary.

The record continues to list the names of the people who
attended the synagogue services. They were from New York,
New Orleans, Savannah, Charleston and Philadelphia. One con-
gregant was from Germany. These people apparently all spent
their vacation in Newport and these services were held only
during the summer. The synagogue was used for services during
the summer and later on the High Holy Days and for other
occasions several times between 1850 and 1883. In 1853 "private
services" were held in the synagogue by Judge Philip J. Joachim-
sen and his family, who "continued to do so every succeeding
Saturday." Similarly in 1863, the family of Lawrence Blumenthal
held private services in the synagogue, and occasionally also
arranged for public services. An interesting entry in the records
of July 26th of that year reads: "L. Blumenthal have again
lamented here in prayers as for several years, the 9th of Abh
being the day of the burning of our Jerusalem and Temple."
During all these services, private or public, memorial prayers
for the members of the Touro family were recited.

Among the visitors to the synagogue in the eight years between 1854 and 1861, the record book reveals that there were 762 Christians and 103 Jews from various parts of the country and from abroad. Among the outstanding events recorded is one which took place on July 12, 1870, when:

> the officers of District Grand Lodge No. 1, I.O.B.B. after having installed the officers of the several B'nai B'rith lodges in the cities of Boston, Mass. & Providence, R.I. made their special business to visit the city & inspecting this sacred place of worship.

In 1858, no less than $4,455.46 was paid out from the *Synagogue Fund* established with the bequest of Abraham Touro by the *General Assembly* in 1823. In 1872, gas lighting was installed in the synagogue, and a permanent custodian was appointed by the *City Council*.[4]

Over the years thousands of Christians and Jews from various parts of the country and from abroad visited the synagogue. They came from all over to view with admiration what a people — once oppressed, persecuted, and haunted by the Inquisition, given the opportunity for freedom — can do and build for the glory of God and for the free exercise of religion according to the dictates of one's conscience.

From Old to New

In the last three decades of the nineteenth century new Jewish residents began to settle in Newport. Again persecution, massacre, discrimination and religious intorelance drove to American shores, peoples of all backgrounds and creeds among them Jews from central and eastern Europe. Some found a haven of freedom and opportunity on the shores of the Narragansett. They became peddlers, small shopkeepers, and workers. Jointly they yearned to manifest their religious faith and communion with God through the synagogue. Before long there were a sufficient number of permanent Jewish residents in the city to form the nucleus of a congregation to worship in the "old" *Touro Synagogue*.[5] As if by the finger of God these new Jewish settlers in Newport came to create the bond betwen them and the old pioneers, to create continuity and immortality. For the continuity to be in spiritual consonance with the earliest founders of the community and synagogue, it had to be in the Sephardic spirit, custom and ritual.

The Spanish-Portuguese Jews and their descendants are very zealous that synagogues founded by them, or in their control, should maintain and uphold the Sephardic tradition in the ritual of the services. The problem of the Sephardic ritual arose in America as early as 1730, when the *Congregation Shearith Israel* in New York was completing its first synagogue on Mill Street. At that time the New York congregation, just as the Newport congregation later, appealed for aid to various other congregations. Amongst them was the congregation of Curaçao, where the Reverend Raphael Jeshurun officiated as *Haham*. We note that when *Haham Jeshurun* sent his collection to New York, he specified definitely:

> Now I must tell you that the Members of this Holy Congregation Whom devotly Contributed to Wards this Benefaction, as they know that the (asquenazum) or Germans, are more in number than Wee there, the desire of you not to Consent not Withstanding they are the most, to Let them have any More Votes nor Authority then they have had hitherto and for the performance of Which you are to get them to Signe an agreement of the Same by all of them, and that one copy of the Sayd agreement Remain in the Hands of Mr. Luis Gomez as the Eldest Member and Another to be Sent to me for the Treasurer of this Congregation to Keep in his Books, and as this request is funded in Solesiting the Peace and Unety of that Holy Congregation I hope that you as Well as the Asquinazim, Whom all I wish God may bless, Will Comply With this my Petition for our devines tells us that the foundation of the Begist Blessing that God found to Bles his dear people was Peace (as it is written) God Bless his People with Peace With which he may Bless and Keep you many years - according to his power -." [6]

The Curaçao congregation, in making its gift, desired definite assurance that the ritual would be maintained according to the traditional Spanish-Portuguese *minhag*.

The same problem seemed to have arisen in regard to the new-born Jewish community in Newport, which was developing rapidly in the latter part of the nineteenth century. This problem was very vexing to the New York congregation, which was zealous to maintain the old form of worship as practiced in the Newport synagogue in the eighteenth century when it was built.

The problem of the ritual was more aggravated because of the current Reform movement, which swept the entire United States. In the second half of the nineteenth century, the Reform movement began to develop in this country, and before long it took root in many old congregations as well as those newly organized. What the traditional Spanish-Portuguese Jew avoids more than Ashkenazic ritual is the Reform movement and the Reform ritual in the synagogue. The Sephardic Jews have always had high regard for the religious traditions and observances in the home and the synagogue that have evolved among Spanish and Portuguese Jews and their decendants, and they never allowed for any changes or deviations, particualrly in the synagogue ritual.

This apprehension moved the *Congregation Shearith Israel* in New York, who was the legal owner and in complete charge of the Newport synagogue, to look with suspicion on the new Jewish community of Newport. Fortunately their suspicion was not well founded, for the new Jewish community was essentially traditional in character, and as eager to preserve traditional Judaism as the Spanish-Portuguese Jews in New York. However, guidance and care on the part of the New Yorkers were nevertheless understandable.

In 1881, the problem of the legal rights of the *Congregation Shearith Israel* in the management and supervision of the *Touro Synagogue* and the old Jewish cemetery in Newport came up and assumed serious proportions. The problem arose with the application to the Newport City Council by the small but growing new Jewish community for the use of the synagogue for religious services and the income from the Touro funds. The *Congregation Shearith Israel,* holding the legal title to the synagogue property, did not desire to deny the Newport Jews the use of the premises or the benefit of the Touro funds. They only feared lest the new Jewish community in Newport, like so many others of the nineteenth century, would not remain Orthodox or would not retain the traditional *Sephardic* custom in the religious worship, which was a condition upon which the use of the synagogue and the income from the Touro funds depended.[7]

As a consequence Gratz Nathan, an attorney and a member of the Board of Trustees of the *Congregation Shearith Israel,* was authorized to ascertain as well as to confirm and assert whatever legal rights the New York congregation had. After having ascertained these rights, Dr. H. Pereira Mendes, the spiritual leader of *Congregation Shearith Israel,* appeared before the Newport City Council on behalf of his congregation. The City Council, upholding the legal rights of the New York congregation, resolved that the application of "the Jews who recently settled in Newport and who desired the use of the synagogue should be transmitted to the *Congregation Shearith Israel* in New York." In consonance with this resolution the new Jewish residents of Newport turned to the *Congregation Shearith Israel* for permission to use the *Touro Synagogue,* to engage a permanent rabbi, and to use the income from the Touro funds to maintain the religious services and the spiritual leadership.[8]

Congregation Shearith Israel received the application favorably and agreed to supply the Newport community with a *Sephardic hazzan* for the High Holy Days. However, they decided not to make the income of the Touro funds available to the Newporters until a permanent congregation was organized to maintain regular services at the *Touro Synagogue* throughout the year "in accordance with the principles and forms of orthodox Judaism so contemplated by the terms of Judah Touro." Thereupon the New York congregation sent to Newport some of the Holy Scrolls that originally belonged to the old Newport congregation, to be used for the High Holy Days. The Reverend Henry Samuel Morais was engaged to conduct the services.[9]

On several occasions before and sporadically after 1881, Dr. Mendes officiated at various services in the *Touro Synagogue.*[10] In 1883, after negotiations with the *Congregation Shearith Israel* in New York, the Newport Jewish community, though not

organized as yet into a congregation, was granted the privilege
to reopen and use the *Touro Synagogue* for permanent public
worship. In order to retain the Spanish-Portuguese ritual in the
synagogue service, Reverend Abraham Pereira Mendes, father
of Dr. H. Pereira Mendes was invited to become the rabbi of
the Newport synagogue.[11]

Rabbi Abraham Pereira Mendes was born in Kingston,
Jamaica. He was trained for the rabbinate and had been preacher
of the Sephardic synagogue in London under the auspices of the
London Sephardic community. For a while he was spiritual
leader of the Ashkenazic community in Birmingham. Later he
was headmaster of the Jews' Hospital and Orphanage, and
directed a school in Northwick Terrace. His chief pride was
that he ministered as a rabbi to the spiritual needs of the Jewish
community in his native city Kingston, Jamaica.[12]

Reconsecration

The first thing Rabbi Mendes did upon assuming the active
ministry in Newport was to arrange for the reconsecration of
the *Touro Synagogue* for permanent worship. The Reconsecration Service took place on May 25, 1883, two hundred and
twenty-five years after the first settlement of the Jews in Newport.

Phoenix-like, Kingston, that harbors the ashes of the minister
that consecrated the synagogue in 1763, supplied the minister to
bring it to life again with the reconsecration, one hundred and
twenty years later. One cannot help but stand in awe and be
inspired by the fact that the ritual of the consecration and the
reconsecration was the same in essence, and the melodies chanted
were almost identical in tune and harmony. The solemnity and
sacredness of the occasion again invited awe and admiration,
though in the congregation of 1883, within the synagogue walls,
the names of Lopez and Rivera, Touro and Alvarez were no
more heard except in memorial prayer.

The Reconsecration Service was graphically described in the
press of the day:

Order of Service

TO BE OBSERVED AT THE

Re-opening of the Touro Synagogue,

NEWPORT, R. I.

on Friday, 19th Iyar 5643.—25th May, 1883.

The persons appointed to carry the Scrolls of the Law, will bring them to the door of the Synagogue.

The minister, preceding them, will then chant:

Minister—: פתחו לנו שערי צדק נבא בם נודה יה

Open to us the gates of righteousness, we will enter them and praise the Lord.

Congregation—: זה השער לה' צדיקים יבאו בו

This is the gate dedicated to the Lord, the righteous shall enter therein.

Having entered, Minister and Congregation chant—

ברוך הבא בשם יי ברכנוכם מבית יי אל יי ויאר לנו : אסרו חג בעבותים עד קרנות המזבח אלי
אתה ואודך אלהי א־רממך : הודו ליי כי טוב כי לעולם חסדו : הודו ליי כי טוב כי לעולם חסדו :

Blessed be he who cometh in the name of the Lord: we bless you from the house of the Lord. God is Lord and He hath enlightened us. Bind the sacrifice with myrtle branches to the horns of the altar. Thou art my Lord, I will praise Thee O my God, I will extol Thee. O give thanks unto the Lord for He is good, for His mercy endureth for ever.

The procession then proceeds to make the circuit of the Synagogue during which the following Psalm is chanted by the Minister and Congregation.

Psalm XXX—מזמור שיר חנופת הבית לדוד וג'

A Psalm and Song of the dedication of the house of David. I will extol thee, O Lord; for thou hast lifted me up, and hast not made my foes to rejoice over me. O Lord my God, I cried unto thee, and thou hast healed me. Oh Lord, thou hast brought up my soul from the grave: thou hast kept me alive, that I should not go down to the pit. Sing unto the Lord, O ye saints of his, and give thanks at the remembrance of his holiness. For his anger endureth but a moment; in his favour is life: weeping may endure for a night, but joy cometh in the morning. And in my prosperity, I said I shall never be moved. Lord, by the favour thou hast made my mountain to stand strong: thou didst hide thy face, and I was troubled. I cried to thee, O Lord; and unto the Lord I made supplication. What profit is there in my blood, when I go down to the pit? Shall the dust praise thee? shall it declare thy truth? Hear, O Lord, and have mercy upon me: Lord, be thou my helper. Thou hast turned for me my mourning into dancing: thou hast put off my sackcloth, and girded me with gladness; To the end that my glory may sing praise to thee, and not be silent. O Lord my God, I will give thanks unto thee for ever

The Minister and bearers of the Scrolls having returned to the Tebah, the following is chanted :—

ימלוך ה' לעולם אלהיך ציון לדור ודור הללו ה :

The Lord shall reign for ever; Thy God, O Zion unto all generations Hallelujah. (repeat)

Psalm XXIX—מזמור לדוד הבו וגו'

A Psalm of David. Give unto the Lord, O ye mighty, give unto the Lord glory and strength. Give unto the Lord the glory due unto his name; worship the Lord in the beauty of holiness. The voice of the Lord is upon the waters: the God of glory thundereth: the Lord is upon many waters. The voice of the Lord is powerful; the voice of the Lord is full of majesty. The voice of the Lord breaketh cedars; yea, the Lord breaketh the cedars of Lebanon. He maketh them also to skip like a calf; Lebanon and Sirion like a young unicorn. The voice of the Lord divideth the flame of fire. The voice of the Lord shaketh the wilderness; the Lord shaketh the wilderness of Kadesh. The voice of the Lord maketh the hinds to calve, and discovereth the forests: and in his temple doth every one speak of his glory. The Lord sitteth upon the flood ; yea, the Lord sitteth King for ever. The Lord will give strength unto his people; the Lord will bless his people with peace.

Prayer for the government.

Prayer in memory of Isaac, Abraham and Judah Touro.

SABBATH EVE SERVICE.

SERMON: by Rev. A. P. Mendes.

Hymn—יגדל אלהים חי - Extolled and praised be the living God.

Order of Service of the Reconsecration of the Touro Synagogue in 1883

The Jewish Synagogue on Touro Street, which has been closed
for a number of years, was re-opened last evening and rededicated,
to public worship with interesting exercises. The Synagogue was
opened to the public and a large congregation assembled to witness
and take part in the services. Many prominent citizens were present and among them were Mayor Franklin, Judge Tillinghast of
the Supreme Court, City Treasurer Coggeshall, several of the clergy-
men of this city and several members of the City Government, Dr.
Henry E. Turner, Mr. George C. Mason, and others.

Rev. de Sola Mendes and Rev. H. P. Mendes brought to the door
of the synagogue the old scrolls of the laws which have been kept
in New York. The minister and the people chanted several verses
and the procession made the circuits of the synagogue. A consecration
prayer was then offered and the scrolls were placed in their appropriate place and the incense lamp was lighted. A prayer in
English was offered and another in memory of Isaac, Abraham and
Judah Touro was offered in Hebrew. The Sabbath eve service was
then conducted by the Rev. H. P. Mendes, the congregation joining
in the Hebrew chants. An excellent sermon was then preached by
the new Minister, Rev. A. P. Mendes, who took for his text, Isaiah,
11:5 "And righteousness shall be the girdle of his loins, and faith-
fulness the girdle of his veins." [13]

In the historic tradition of the *Touro Synagogue* and the old
Jewish community of Newport, Rabbi Mendes carried out a program of good will and understanding between all citizens and
creeds in the city. He lectured before church groups; presented a
historic paper on the old cemetery before the *Newport Historical
Society* membership; invited the Jewish personnel of the *Naval
Training Stations* to the synagogue; arranged for the Passover
observance for the Jewish personnel in the armed services, and
generally promoted and advanced the ideals of brotherhood in
the community.[14]

Rabbi Abraham Pereira Mendes met with a fatal street
accident in New York City. He passed away on April 4, 1893.

By the time of the passing of Rabbi Mendes, the new Jewish
community of Newport had not as yet formed a permanent congregation. The problem now arose as to the organization of
such a congregation. The Jewish people in Newport were
divided in their opinion as to the nature of this new congregation,

and which of the Jewish residents should constitute this new body. Two distinct groups evolved. Each aimed to use the *Touro Synagogue* for services and the income from the Touro funds for its budgetary expenses of maintaining the synagogue, the services, the Religious School and the ministry.[15]

The authority of *Shearith Israel* of New York over the Newport synagogue was challenged time and time again by the two groups. "More than once" writes Dr. Pool:

> representatives of the *Shearith Israel Congregation* had presented before the Newport City Council or Rhode Island House of Representative in Providence, memorandums about *Shearith Israel's* rights over the Newport synagogue and cemetery, particularly as to the control of the "character of the synagogue's ritual and ministry." [16]

On June 13, 1893, the Board of Trustees of the *Congregation Shearith Israel* of New York were the recipients of a communication from the Reverend David Baruch, whom they had appointed as the *hazzan* of the Newport synagogue to succeed Rabbi Abraham Pereira Mendes, to the following effect: "Two separate bodies had organized at that place, each claiming to exercise authority over the Synagogue and appurtenances, one of which had applied to the Legislature for a charter." [17] The group that applied for a charter for a permanent congregation decided to call itself *Congregation Jeshuat Israel*.[18]

The *Congregation Shearith Israel* of New York, anticipating the granting of the charter to the new *Congregation Jeshuat Israel* reassured its legal rights to the *Touro Synagogue* with an act of conveyance or "Deed of Trust," which the remaining legal heirs of the old synagogue in Newport made to them in April, 1894. This not only reaffirmed the right of the *Congregation Shearith Israel* in the trusteeship and control they had held with relation to the synagogue for practically a century, but also definitely determined the nature of the worship and the ritual that must be observed in this historic edifice.

In this "Deed of Trust" the conveyers definitely specified that they gave the synagogue:

herein above described and every part thereof, to use and apply the
same, or cause the same to be used, occupied and employed for the
maintenance therein of the usual and stated Religious services according to the Ritual, Rites, and Customs of the Orthodox Spanish
and Portuguese Jews, as at the time practiced and observed in the
Synagogue of this Congregation Shearith Israel in the City of New
York now located at No. 5 West 19th Street in Said City.[19]

When the charter for the new congregation was granted
by the Legislature on June 13, 1894, it provided in Section I:

Eugene Schreier, Giacomo Servadio, Louis Hess, Henry Hess, Isaac
Bergman, Julius Engel, Israel J. Josephson, Alfred Schreier, their
associates and successors, are hereby made a corporation by the
name of the Congregation Jeshuat Israel, for the purpose of religious
worship, in the city of Newport, according to the Sephardic Ritual
and strict rules and laws of the orthodox Jewish Faith.[20]

To comply with this condition, the constitution of *Congregation Jeshuat Israel* stipulated:

The Ritual and customs of this Congregation shall forever remain
according to the Sephardic Minhag, as at present practiced and constituted in this Congregation.

The bond between *Congregation Jeshuat Israel* and the *Congregation Shearith Israel* was strengthened by the further provision in the constitution which combined the two congregations
almost physically:

The government of this congregation shall be vested in the President and three Trustees elected by this Congregation, and four
Trustees appointed by the Spanish and Portuguese Congregation
Shearith Israel of New York City, who shall be guided in all
spiritual affairs by such laws as are now in force or may hereafter
be adopted by this Congregation, and have the arrangements of all
temporal matters appertaining to the Congregation and School connected thereto.

To further strengthen this bond, the constitution also provided that:

No addition, alteration, or amendment shall be made to this
Constitution and By-Laws that shall in any way add to, alter or
affect the status of the four Trustees of the Spanish and Portuguese
Congregational (sic.) Shearith Israel of the City of New York, or

of Article XIX of this Constitution and By-Laws, unless the said four Trustees of the said Congregation Shearith Israel vote affirmatively for such proposed addition, alteration or amendment.[21]

When more than half a century later, a new set of By-Laws was adopted by the *Congregation Jeshuat Israel,* the first article was careful to state:

> This Congregation shall be known by the name: The Congregation Jeshuat Israel (K.K.) as provided by Certificates of Incorporation as enacted by the General Assembly on the 13th day of June, 1894, for the purpose of religious worship in the City of Newport, according to the Sephardic Ritual and strict rules and laws of the Orthodox Jewish Faith, with all the powers and privileges, and subject to all the duties and liabilities, set forth in Chapter 152 of the Public Statutes and in any acts in amendment thereof or in addition thereto.[22]

Problems of Adjustment

The newly organized *Congregation Jeshuat Israel* obtained the privilege of holding its services at the old synagogue on a dollar-a-year lease and of applying the proceeds of the *Judah Touro Ministerial Fund* for the upkeep of its minister, religious services and school. The Reverend David Baruch officially became the *hazzan* of the new *Congregation Jeshuat Israel.* Thus not only were the old synagogue and its services revived as had been the dream of the Touros, but the new congregation bore the same name as the old one.

The Reverend David Baruch was born in Amsterdam, Holland on April 19, 1847. He was of Sephardic origin and conducted the services at the synagogue according to the Sephardic ritual and in the Sephardic pronunciation, as had Rabbi Mendes.

On March 30, 1899, the Reverend David Baruch was gathered to his fathers. The Reverend Abraham H. Nieto, associate *hazzan* of the Spanish-Portuguese Synagogue of New York officiated.

In the meantime the other of the two groups alluded to before continued its organization, even after the Legislature had granted the charter to the *Congregation Jeshuat Israel.* This group functioned and held services under the name of *Touro Congregation.* The services of the *Touro Congregation* were held in private houses. Occasionally during a holiday, the rooms at the old City Hall - the present Chamber of Commerce, one of the historic buildings of the City of Newport - were rented for public worship.

On April 10, 1899, the *Touro Congregation* obtained a corporate charter from the Rhode Island Legislature "for the purpose of religious worship, according to the rites of the Jewish religion." The charter members were Israel J. Josephson, Barney W. Wilsker, David Frant, Sigmund Barber, Sigmund Schwartz and Moses Wagner.

Upon the death of the Reverened Mr. Baruch, the *Touro Congregation* elected as its *hazzan* the Reverend E. M. Myer. The *Congregation Jeshuat Israel* elected Moses Guedalia. Because the *Touro Congregation* constituted a larger membership, the Council of the City of Newport voted the salary from the *Judah Touro Ministerial Fund* to the Reverend E. M. Myer.[23]

This situation was again a challenge to *Congregation Shearith Israel* in New York. According to Dr. Pool, the controversies and conflicts:

> were due both to the zeal of some individuals in Newport who desired to assume independent control of the synagogue and its administration, and to some actions of Newport's city council in acting as if their being trustees of the Touro Funds gave them rights to the Newport synagogue property. As a result of court action, the city council authorized the complete restoration of all rights in the synagogue to *Congregation Shearith Israel* through its president and representative, L. Napoleon Levy. The New York congregation assumed the court action's costs that ordinarily should have been paid by the losing side, in order to encourage them to attend the services in the synagogue and to co-operate with the synagogue authorities.[24]

Again, it seems, Dr. H. Pereira Mendes effected an inner peace among the contending groups in Newport, even as the civil authorities established the legal rights of the groups and of the *Congregation Shearith Israel.*[25] During the summer of 1899, both congregations "Jeshuat Israel" and "Touro" joined together in worship at the old synagogue. Dr. Mendes, who was spending the summer in Newport, conducted the services. During the High Holy Days of the year 1899, the Reverend E. M. Myer officiated. Subsequently, Mr. Myer was appointed officially to succeed the Reverend Mr. Baruch.

The controversy between the *Congregation Jeshuat Israel* and *Touro Congregation* was only temporarily settled at this time. The harmony and peace achieved did not last long. After a brief interval, the controversy between the *Touro Congregation* and the *Congregation Jeshaut Israel* was again renewed. Each claimed the privilege of using the *Touro Synagogue* for services and to have the rights to the use of the Touro funds. The *Touro Congregation* decided to hold separate services at 11 Coddington Street. For the High Holy Days, they made use again of the rooms of the old City Hall.[26] The differences between the two congregations attracted city-wide attention. Again the *Congregation Shearith Israel* of New York became involved. The problem as far as *Shearith Israel* was concerned was aggravated additionally because of *Congregation Jeshuat Israel's* dollar-a-year lease from *Congregation Shearith Israel* for the use of the synagogue, which the former occasionally failed to honor.[27]

After much controversy and misunderstanding, in which the members of the *Congregation Jeshuat Israel* and the *Touro Congregation* as well as the *Congregation Shearith Israel* of New York participated, the matter came to a truce on April 25, 1902. The two Newport congregations united to worship and to function together under the old name *Congregation Jeshuat Israel*, and to hold services in the historic synagogue, the trusteeship of which remained vested with the *Congregation Shearith Israel* of New York. Hebrew and Sunday School classes were held in the side building adjacent to the synagogue.

By 1903,

the rights of *Shearith Israel* "as the proper successor of the ancient Hebrew congregation at Newport, R. I." has been given recognition beyond question, together with a perpetual guardianship of the synagogue and the land on which it stands: "to use and apply the same, or cause the same to be used, occupied and employed for the maintenance therein of the usual and stated religious services according to the ritual, rites and customs of the orthodox Spanish and Portuguese Jews as at the time practised and observed in the synagogue of the Congregaiton Shearith Israel in the City of New York." [28]

The Reverend E. M. Myer did not stay long in Newport. To succeed him the Reverend Henry Samuel Morais, who officiated at the *Touro Synagogue* during the High Holy Days of the year 1881, was elected to the ministry of the Newport synagogue in 1900.

The Reverend Mr. Morais was born in Philadelphia of Sephardic parents. His father, Rabbi Sabato Morais, founder of the Jewish Theological Seminary of America, came from Italy. Mr. Morais received his Hebrew education from his father. For about twelve years he was instructor in the schools of the *Hebrew Education Society* as well as in the *Hebrew Sabbath Schools* in Philadelphia. He was the founder and editor of the *Jewish Exponent* and of *The Hebrew Watchword and Instructor.* He contributed frequently to the general and Jewish press in the United States. In 1897-8, Morais was acting minister of the *Congregation Mikveh Israel* of Philadelphia. In 1899-1900, he held the position of minister of the *Congregation Adath Jeshurun* of Syracuse, New York. It was from there that he received the call to come to Newport, where he officiated during the year 1900-1. Morais was the author of two books published prior to his coming to Newport: *Eminent Israelites of the Nineteenth Century* and *The Jews of Philadelphia.*[29]

Reverend Henry S. Morais was the last of the Sephardic ministers who served the *Touro Synagogue.* It is to be noted that not all ministers of the *Touro Synagogue* were ordained rabbis even though most assumed the title rabbi. Some were only *hazzanim* or cantors, who ministered in whatever capacity suitable. The same situation prevailed among the Ashkenazic spiritual leaders that followed Morais. Some were ordained rabbis, some were only cantors.

In 1902, Jacob M. Seidel was called to the ministry of the congregation. He was an ordained rabbi, the first Ashkenazic spirtual leader of the Newport congregation. The services at the synagogue continued in the Sephardic ritual, however, but not as regards the Spanish-Portuguese pronunciation of the Hebrew.[30]

Rabbi Seidel was succeeded in his ministry in 1905 by Cantor Maurice Kaplan. During Cantor Kaplan's ministry the *Congregation Jeshuat Israel* attempted to make certain alterations and additions to the side building where the religious school was conducted. As this could not be done without the consent of the Board of Trustees of the *Congregation Shearith Israel,* a letter was dispatched to New York addressed to Dr. H. Pereira Mendes asking for permission. When Dr. Mendes presented the letter before the Board of his congregation on February 27, 1905, the result recorded in the minutes was obvious:

> Communication received from Congregation Jeshuat Israel, Newport, R.I. (addressed to the Minister) relative to altering Synagogue at Newport for additional school rooms and Reverend Mr. Mendes was directed to reply that this Board would not consent to any alteration of any description in that historic edifice.[31]

The *Congregation Shearith Israel* of New York was interested to preserve not only the historic religious tradition of the Newport synagogue, but also the physical structure itself. The synagogue in Newport was to remain unaltered both physically and spiritually.

The Newport congregation accepted this justifiable ruling and arranged to take care of its Religious School in the facilities extant.

By this time the synagogue at Newport was restored to its ancient foundations in all aspects. As in the days of yore, the beautiful Psalms were sung in the traditional Sephardic chants. In the building on the side, religious instruction was given to the Jewish youth of Newport. To complete the organization of the Jewish community the *Ladies' Auxiliary of the Congregation Jeshuat Israel* was organized, taking for its aim: "the support and temporary help of the poor and sick, visiting the poor of a deserving nature, and to see to the maintenance of a regular and well established Hebrew and Religious School."[32]

Before a decade of the new century had passed, the three foundations, of the Jewish world, *Torah* - education, *Avodah* - religious service, and *Gmiluth Chasadim* - beneficence, again emanated from the portals of the old shrine - the historic synagogue in Newport.

Chapter 9

AND REMEMBERED BE FOR GOOD

SINCE all inner and outer conflicts in the community had been settled and the ritual, ownership and supervision of the *Touro Synagogue* had been finally established, the *Congregation Jeshuat Israel* was able to strengthen its position in the city and concentrate on its growth and development. Reverend Maurice Kaplan was succeeded in the pulpit of the *Touro Synagogue* by Rabbi Bernard H. Rosengard. Rabbi Rosengard continued the Sephardic tradition in the religious services. He was also cognizant of the fact that the *Touro Synagogue* is a historic landmark.

A historic landmark lends itself to many anniversaries. The *Touro Synagogue,* because of its background and colorful history and the many and various historic events associated with it, certainly lent itself to many anniversaries.

When Rabbi Abraham Pereira Mendes passed away, an artistic wooden tablet to his sacred memory was dedicated on the synagogue premises. The tablet read:

And God said unto him
Abraham:
and he said Behold, here I am
In Memoriam of
REV. ABRAHAM PEREIRA MENDES
Born Kingston, Jamaica, on
ROSH HODESH ADAR 5585. 19th February 1825

Died in the City of New York, on
18th Nisan 5653. 4th April 1893
May his soul rest in peace, Amen
Erected by the Members of the
Congregation Jeshuat Israel

In 1908, a quarter of a century after the reconsecration of
the synagogue by Rabbi Abraham Pereira Mendes, it was an
opportune occasion for an anniversary celebration. By this time
the wooden tablet was found to be weather-worn and inadequate.
Rabbi Rosengard therefore decided to arrange for the observance
of the twenty-fifth anniversary of the reconsecration of the *Touro
Synagogue* by erecting and dedicating a new tablet commemorating not only Rabbi A. P. Mendes, but also the names of those
who were instrumental in the original dedication of the synagogue in 1763, and the preservation and maintenance of the
synagogue during the nineteenth century. Accordingly a marble
tablet was erected on the western wall, bearing the inscription:

IN MEMORIAM
REVEREND ISAAC TOURO
Rabbi of this Synagogue from its dedication
5523-1763 until the American Revolution
Born 5498-1738
Died Tebet 14, 5544 - December 8, 1783

ABRAHAM
Son of REV. ISAAC TOURO
Born in Newport 5534 - 1774
Died Heshvan 6, 5583 - October 18, 1822

JUDAH
Son of REV. ISAAC TOURO
Born in Newport, Sivan 18, 5535 - June 16, 1775
Died Tebet 18, 5614 - January 13, 1854
Their sacred gifts endowed this Holy Sanctuary

REVEREND ABRAHAM PEREIRA MENDES
Rabbi of this Synagogue
5641 - 1881[1] — 5653 - 1893
Born R. H. Ve Adar 5585 - February 19, 1825
Died Nissan 18, 5653 - April 4, 1893
The fruit of the righteous is a tree of life;
And he that winneth souls is wise.

Proverbs XI:30

The ceremony of the dedication of the tablet to the four "pillars" of the synagogue was an impressive climax to the story of the old Jewish community and its transition to the new. The synagogue was decorated with flowers and palms and illuminated with burning candles from the old candelabra. It was Monday, September 7, 1908. The synagogue was filled to capacity, much before the time set for the beginning of the ceremonies. Within the Reading-desk enclosure were seated Rabbi B. H. Rosengard and Dr. David de Sola Pool. Among those in the synagogue were the mayor and other public officials of city and state and the non-Jewish clergy.

The principal address was delivered by the then curator of the *American Jewish Historical Society,* Leon Huhner.

Among other remarks of a historic nature Mr. Huhner pointed out:

> To the Jew, Newport has always been a cherished name, for here it was that civil and religious liberty were first firmly established by that illustrious champion of brotherhood of man, Roger Williams. Like the great temple in Rome dedicated to all the gods, so Rhode Island became the Pantheon for all sects and all creeds irrespective of race or nation.
>
> Nor did the Jews abuse this liberality, for nowhere did they have a prouder record of the past than in this very city. While found as pioneers in each of the thirteen original colonies, it may fairly be said that nowhere did they exert greater or more beneficial influence than in Colonial Newport.[2]

Following the address, the Honorable N. Taylor Phillips, a descendant of the Revolutionary patriot Jonas Phillips, drew the curtain which unveiled the white marble tablet bearing the inscription in gold letters. Before the unveiling of the tablet Captain Phillips spoke briefly on the historic associations between the *Congregation Jeshuat Israel* of Newport and the *Congregation Shearith Israel* of New York. The tablet was presented to the City of Newport as the custodians of the *Holy Building*. On behalf of the city, Mayor William P. Clarke, accepted the tablet with a brief address, expressing the joy of the city in preserving such records of historic association and significance. The memorial prayer for those commemorated on the tablet was then offered by Dr. Pool. This was followed by an address by the Reverend Emery H. Porter, who brought greetings in the name of the clergy of the City. Rabbi Rosengard closed the exercise with the priestly benediciton.[3]

Rabbi Rosengard ministered to *Congregation Jeshuat Israel* until 1909. He was succeeded in 1910, by Rabbi Benjamin A. Lichter, who ministered until 1912. Rabbi Lichter was the first rabbi of the *Touro Synagogue* who was a graduate of an American Seminary. He had graduated the Jewish Theological Seminary the year he assumed the position in Newport. During that year also Reverend Nathan Friedman became the Reader and Cantor of the synagogue. Reverend Mr. Friedman actively served the congregation thirty-six years, until 1946, when he became emeritus. He passed away May 29, 1948.

After Rabbi Lichter, Rabbis Aaron Shappo (1921), Abraham Bengis (1921), and Alter Abelson (1926-27); and Cantors Julius Bloch (1912-18), David Brodsky (1919-21), and Sol Bailey (1922-25), ministered at the *Touro Synagogue*. In 1928, Rabbi Jacob Seidel was recalled to the pulpit. Rabbi Seidel resigned his position in 1932, when he was succeeded by Rabbi Morris A. Gutstein, who graduated that year from the Jewish Theological Seminary, and who ministered to the spiritual needs of the *Touro Synagogue* and the Jewish community of Newport until 1943, when he left for Chicago, Illinois.

Following Rabbi Gutstein, Rabbi Jules Lipschutz, a graduate of the *Rabbi Isaac Elchanan Theological Seminary* became the spiritual leader of the *Congregation Jeshuat Israel,* and Reverend Ely Katz became its cantor. In 1949, Rabbi Lipschutz was succeeded in the pulpit by Rabbi Theodore Lewis from Ireland, the present spiritual leader.[4]

Four Anniversaries

The year 1933 was another occasion for a gala anniversary celebration of that historic shrine. In May of that year it was fifty years since the *Touro Snagogue* was reopened and reconsecrated for permanent worship. It was also the two hundred and seventy-fifth year of the first settlement of the Jews in Newport; the one hundred and seventieth year of the dedication of the synagogue; and the fortieth year of the organization of the new *Congregation Jeshuat Israel.*

Thus, in 1933, a four-fold anniversary commemorating these events centered around the *Touro Synagogue.*

This four-fold anniversary was celebrated with various impressive ceremonies from Friday evening, May 26th to Sunday evening, May 28th. It attracted nation-wide as well as city-wide attention. The first event of the anniversary was an impressive *Sabbath Eve Service.*

The Rev. Dr. H. Pereira Mendes, then eighty-one years old, who fifty years before had the privilege to coofficiate with his father Rabbi A. Pereira Mendes at the reconsecration of the synagogue, preached the sermon.

Dr. Mendes was deeply moved at the thought of preaching from the same pulpit his father did. He took for his text the same Biblical verse from Isaiah that his father used in 1883 at the Reconsecration Service. Then he interpreted the verse from Numbers 1:2 and said:

> What is the meaning of "Stand by your flag?" We have done so in ten thousand places. God calls upon us to call mankind to God. This is and means our responsibility, standing by our flag. God leads us and sees us scattered over the world. There must be a divine purpose in that. God desires that we benefit all nations of the world.
> Why have you all come to America? You are here in order to

bring into our national life and into our personal lives a truer and greater consciousness of God.[5]

The second event of this four-fold anniversary was the *Sabbath Morning Service* at which Dr. David de Sola Pool preached the sermon.

Dr. Pool gave a short résumé of the settlement of the Jews in North America and the history of the *Touro Synagogue*. He pointed out the close association of his congregation, which was founded in 1654, and the Newport Jewish community founded four years later. He referred to the *Touro Synagogue* as "The American Synagogue" in the truest sense of the word. He then called attention to the ideals of religious liberty that were pronounced through this synagogue on many occasion by many personalities including the father of our country, George Washington, and suggested that Americanism and Judaism can thus be linked spiritually. Dr. Pool concluded that the synagogue must be made the center of all religious and cultural community living, in order to assert its historic role and preserve Jewish community life.[6]

Four anniversary functions took place during the day on Sunday, May 28th. In the morning a special *Children's Service* was held. Following this service the parents took their children to be blessed by the eighty-one year old esteemed Rabbi Mendes.

In the early afternoon, Dr. Gutstein delivered an Anniversary Address over radio station W.P.R.O. In this address he said in part:

> When the prophet Zechariah beheld the vision of the golden candelabrum of the Beth Hamikdash, the holy Temple in Jerusalem, and the two olive trees one upon the right side and one upon the left side thereof, and he inquired, "What are these my Lord?" he was answered, "This is the word of the Lord. Not by virtue of material strength, nor by political power, shall ye prevail; but by My spirit, saith the Lord of Hosts."
>
> The history of the Jews constitutes an itinerary of a group that is constantly meeting foe and opposition. If the law of the survival of the strongest is applicable to nations, then Israel is certainly an exception to the rule. For no people of whom history makes mention

has suffered so much as the Jews have suffered, and none have clung
with such undying tenacity to the faith of their fathers and the traditions of their faith. Though cast into the four corners of the universe,
driven from continent to continent, subject all over to the massacre
and bloodshed of the violent mobs, and organized persecution, by the
powerful and supposedly civilized rulers, the Jews have yet maintained
themselves as a continuous ethnic group, have retained their identity,
and continued their culture in spite of these many destructive forces.
Fire and famine, sword and dungeon, the rack and gibbet, and
every other machination of torture that hellish vengeance and persecution could devise, have held no terrors for our ancestors who,
with a smile on their dark faces went forth to their inevitable doom,
with their last dying glance looking proudly to Heaven, murmuring
silently: "Hear O Israel the Eternal is our God the Eternal is one."

One might well ask "What is it that kept and still keeps Israel together and ensures its existence? To this the answer can be only: "Not
by material strength nor by political power, but by My spirit saith
the Lord of Hosts," the spirit of God as it reveals itself through
Torah; the spirit of Torah as it reveals itself through Israel; and
the spirit of Israel as it reveals itself through the synagogue; the
spirit which the rabbis of old so beautifully termed: "the Holy One
blessed be He-God, Torah, and Israel are unique." It was this spirit
that prevailed among the Jewish pioneers in America, particularly
in Newport, Rhode Island, who when they arrived in the year
1658, they brought with themselves, not material wealth, nor political
power, but the spirit of God, a Holy Scroll - a Torah - that they
salvaged from the Spanish Inquisition and carried it with them
throughout their wandering. And when those saintly persons came
to Newport, the first thing they did was to establish a congregation,
which according to tradition they called with this beautiful name,
true to the spirit of liberty and freedom implanted in this colony
by its father, Roger Williams, *Yeshuat Israel - Salvation of Israel*.[7]

The climactic event in the entire celebration was the special
Anniversary Service in the midafternoon. At this service the
Reconsecration Service conducted by Rabbi Abraham P. Mendes
was reenacted. The synagogue was filled to capacity with an
overflowing audience crowding the synagogue lawn and the side-
walks when the solemn service began. Among the audience were
present many dignitaries of the City, State and Church.

Addressing the large Christian representation present, Dr.

Mendes, at the close of his address, according to the report in
the press:

> asked his Christian hearers, to consider what would be the reception
> that their leader, the Nazarene, would receive should he return to
> this earth today and prosecute his missions of healing the sick;
> giving sight to the blind; hearing to the deaf; relief to the maimed;
> and consolation to the bereaved; should he pass along the streets
> of Germany today? In ringing words he answered his own question
> saying he would be crushed, and forbidden to proceed, and would
> finally be driven from the country. Why? Because of his good
> work? No! But because his mother was a Jewess! Think of it, con-
> sider it! A dramatic sensation was created, filled by a silence in
> which the dropping of a pin could have been heard. The impres-
> sion made was indelible.[8]

Mayor Mortimer A. Sullivan presented greetings on behalf
"of all of the races of Newport." Among other things, the
mayor said:

> Cities, states and nations have characters like individuals and
> their actions are reflected likewise to build reputations. Newport's
> reputation has been built in a large measure by the people of your
> faith. Our colony founded on religious freedom in 1639 has ever
> kept faith.
>
> Today in our great depression we find economic and social rules
> predominating. But I assure you that when the people return to the
> law of Moses and the Ten Commandments, no other regulations for
> peoples and nations will be necessary. I like to think of those men
> of your religion who gave so much to the development of our
> nation. Your position in our community is secure.[9]

Following the Anniversary Service the people, led by Dr.
Mendes and Dr. Gutstein dressed in their rabbinic robes, moved
in procession from the synagogue to the old Jewish cemetery,
where *Memorial Services* were held for the early Jewish pioneers
and settlers, who are interred in the historic *Abode of Life*. Dr.
Mendes chanted the memorial prayers in the traditional Sephardic
contents, tune and pronunciation. Dr. Gutstein delivered the
eulogy paying tribute to the founders of the Jewish community,
to the builders of the synagogue, and to those who endowed the
old historic landmarks which made possible their preservation
for posterity.[10]

Three Centuries of Freedom

Three years after this gala four-fold anniversary, in 1936, the State of Rhode Island celebrated its Tercentenary. It was only natural that the *Touro Synagogue,* that occupies such a glorious place in the history of the State, should be the scene of an important event in this Tercentenary celebration. July 5th of that year was proclaimed by Governor Theodore Francis Green as "Jewish Day." In making this proclamation the governor wrote:

> The laudable desire of the Jewish citizenry of Rhode Island to devote this day to a celebration of our three centuries of progress, is quite understandable merely as an expression of civic pride. It achieves greater brilliance of meaning when one considers the appropriateness of an especial day celebration because of the relation between the founding of the State and the history of the Jews here.[11]

In conjunction with the Jewish Day celebration the *Zionist Organization of America* decided to hold its national convention that year in Providence. On July 5, 1936, the delegates to the convention coming from all the states of the union gathered in and outside of the *Touro Synagogue* to join in the celebration of the Rhode Island Tercentenary. It was indeed a momentous occasion when representatives of all American Jewry gathered to offer gratitude to God for religious liberty and freedom that was introduced in the colonies with the establishment of Rhode Island by Roger Williams in 1636.

Mayor Henry S. Wheeler of the City of Newport welcomed the "Members and Friends of the Zionist Convention" in a formal published declaration:

> From the very beginning of Roger Williams' "Livelie Experiment" in Rhode Island, our state has been dedicated to the principle "that none bee accounted a delinquent for doctrine, provided it bee not directly repugnant to ye Government and lawes established." People of your faith can look back to a record of achievement in this State from the day that the first Jew arrived from Portugal in 1658. Few remain who are descendants of the early Jewish settlers, but such names as Touro, Lopez, Pollock, Hays, Levi,

Seixas and other have come down through the years as a lasting memorial to those of the Jewish faith in the early years of our settlement. Their influence upon our young colony was marked and that same influence by the people of your faith continues to be carried on in Newport and in Rhode Island.[12]

The principal address was presented by Dr. Louis Finkelstein, Chancellor and Professor of Theology of the *Jewish Theological Seminary of America.*

Professor Finkelstein held the audience spellbound with his scholarly address. He compared the "livlie experiment" in democracy by Roger Williams to the "Jewish experiment" in religion throughout known history. "One must supplement the other, one cannot be lived adequately by American Jews without the other."

Dr. Finkelstein compared the history of Rhode Island with the history of Judaism and pointed out that both stood guard for centuries over the disciplines that each preached: Rhode Island, liberty and equality; Judaism, law and ethics. "It is therefore little wonder" said Dr. Finkelstein, "that the founding fathers of the United States of America found so much inspiration in the spiritual foundation of the Jewish people, the Hebrew Scriptures." [13]

The Jewish community of Newport joined in other Tercentenary celebrations of Rhode Island during the year. A literary contribution to the Rhode Island Tercentenary was the publication of a book in 1936, dealing with the historic role of the Jews in Colonial Newport, the significance of the *Touro Synagogue* in American history, and the record of the Jewish contribution to Rhode Island's experiment in democracy. It was *The Story of the Jews in Newport* written by Rabbi Morris A. Gutstein.[14]

In this book Rabbi Gutstein traced the background of the coming of the Jews to the New World and their settlement in North America, in New York in 1654 and in Newport in 1658. The author then proceeded to give a documented history of the evolution of the Jewish community of Newport and the building of the *Touro Synagogue,* tracing the events up to 1908, and

Participants in the
Observance of the Newport Tercentenary
in the Touro Synagogue, 1939

Presentation of Book Aaron Lopez and Judah Touro by
Judge Robert M. Dannin to Mayor Henry S. Wheeler, 1939

Service of Intercession on behalf of Jews persecuted
by Nazis, 1940

making it an account of two and a half centuries of Judaism.

Appraising this contribution to the now national historic shrine, the *Touro Synagogue,* Dr. Pool, in the introduction to the book, stated:

> The Jew walks through Touro Street in Newport quietly conscious of inheriting a tradition both of American political and religious liberty and of Jewish idealism and religious faith. The synagogue, which has stood for one and three quarter centuries and which has withstood the alarms of war and the fatalities of swiftly changing time, is a witness of Newport's liberality of spirit and reverence for the ancient Bible, and Israel's loyalty to the teachings which it has borne on its centuried pilgrimage to the four corners of the earth. The quiet God's acre in which lies the dust of Newport's Jews of Colonial days speaks of the identification of the Jew with American life for well nigh three centuries since sturdy Jewish pioneers threw in their lot with their fellow Americans in wresting from the wildernes a settlement of security and refuge for those of all denominations and races seeking ampler living . . .
>
> This is the story which Rabbi Gutstein sets out to tell. It is one that is well worth the telling. It is a brilliant tale in which we meet dignified hidalgos bearing such sun-warmed names as Rodrigues Rivera, Lopez or Touro, working, playing, and praying harmoniously with their brethren from bleaker climes who bear such names as Pollock, Myers or Hart. It is a record which recalls to life the victims of medieval persecution, and the romance of their martyred faith hidden in the untouchable recesses of their soul until in Rhode Island's freedom the cherished faith could again be avowed in light and liberty . . .
>
> This record needs the more to be recited at this time in mankind's history when in the Old World against which America rebelled, systems of nationalistic living are being set up which give to bigotry governmental sanction and to persecution governmental assistance. These twentieth century concepts of the State ruthlessly reject as excessively kindly and compromising even that toleration which George Washington rejected as insufficiently kindly and as incommensurate with the dignity of selfhood and the nobility of the human spirit. If we would preserve our American tradition from contamination by perverted nationalism, we must study such records of our past as this story of Newport in order to understand how strong and how lifegiving are the roots of American democracy and American liberty of the spirit . . . [15]

Dr. Stephen B. Luce, the president of the Newport Historical Society, in commenting upon the book, wrote:

> Such books will go far to bridge the gap between Christian and Jew, and remove the suspicion that each often feels toward the other. In these days when there is so much misunderstanding and hostility between the two creeds in various parts of the so-called civilized world, it is a good thing for us to recall the intimacy of relations and mutual respect that existed between the Lopez, Rivera, Touro, and Seixas families and their Christian neighbors. The scrupulous honesty, integrity, and philanthropy of these men, and the purity of their characters and religious instincts is a part of the common heritage of every Newporter.[16]

Chapter 10

A MONUMENT TO LIBERTY AND
A NATIONAL SHRINE

IN 1939 the City of Newport celebrated the three hundredth anniversary of its founding. It was a celebration, in truth, of three centuries of freedom. For three hundred years in one city uninterruptedly, children of men have lived as children of God should live, side by side as brethren, everyone contributing a share to the welfare of society and all collectively serving God and fellowmen, respecting each other's religious, spiritual, and cultural heritage. Such an anniversary called for gratitude to God and gratitude for man's high ideals of liberty, equality and democracy.

Tercentenary Services

The Jews of Newport were always conscious of this gratitude. They had never forgotten the hospitality they received in that "Commonwealth" and "Democracie," which gave them a haven for freedom.

In consonance with the spirit of the *Touro Synagogue,* the most appropriate way to express this gratitude was by prayer of thanksgiving and praise to God for the bounties of religious freedom, political democracy, and economic opportunity that envolved from the founding of Newport. Accordingly, most picturesque and impressive Tercentenary religious services were held at the *Touro Synagogue* on June 23-24, 1939, marking

131

"the contribution of the Jewish residents of the city toward Newport's Tercentenary observance and commemorating the significance of civic and religious liberty." [1]

Dressed in formal attire, the clergy and lay leaders marched in procession Friday evening into the synagogue to commence the Jewish observance of Newport's Tercentenary. Special prayers were offered for the City, State and Federal governments. Memorial prayers were chanted for the founders of the city, for the early Jewish pioneers, and for the builders of the synagogue. The principal address of the evening was delivered by Dr. David de Sola Pool.

Dr. Pool paid tribute to Newport, saying among other things:

Roger Williams, John Clarke, and Isaac Touro were refugees from oppression. They came here and found liberty.

Here in Newport in 300 years there has been made possible a liberty that is rarely found. You have lived this liberty. This is no provincial celebration.

The test of tolerance is the way the majority treats the minority.

It is not what the Jew has received from America, that we should emphasize. It is what he has given. The synagogue has given to the Protestant and Catholic much of their services. The Jew came like Roger Williams in quest of religious liberty. Of all the groups that have come to America none more than the Jew has learned to love democracy, and appreciate liberty.

Men without religion are destroying Europe today. This vile spirit will destroy America unless we stand together, in our love for democracy and appreciation of liberty.[2]

Then Dr. Pool continued:

The Jews have been identified with the history of Newport well nigh three centuries. They have entered into the very fabric and spirit of its life from the beginning.

Citizens by right together with their Christian fellow citizens they helped develop the spirit of democracy in the state of Roger Williams.

They have testified to the reality of religious liberty and though a numerical minority they have always lived at peace and in fine fellowship with their Christian neighbors. Though few in number they contributed to Newport and American life a passion for human freedom and human rights.

Under American democracy they have lived without constraint. The cause of the American Revolution - Liberty - was the cause which meant life to American Jews and to Judaism.[3]

Greetings on behalf of the city were given by Mayor Henry S. Wheeler. Mayor Wheeler thanked the members of the Jewish faith for their contribution to the city's Tercentenary observance and then continued to point out:

This service exemplifies Newport's spirit of religious tolerance and its broad attitude toward the liberty of conscience. Since the days of the early Jewish pioneers men and women of their faith have helped Newport to steer its course of progress.[4]

Dr. J. Harlow Graham, president of the Newport Ministers Union, speaking on behalf of the non-Jewish clergy in the city, said:

If liberty is to live, the churches and the synagogues must go on as far as possible working together, to build values high, sacred, and lasting. If we do not use our right to worship we are being untrue to the rights of liberty, but if we do, we will go forward in the name of God for the great cause which we have given our lives to.[5]

Other speakers were Canon Stanley C. Hughes, D. D., Rector of the Trinity Church, who spoke on behalf of the Newport churches, and the Honorable Joseph H. Gainer, former Mayor of the City of Providence, who spoke on behalf of Providence Plantations.

Dr. Hughes among other things said:

It is a pleasure to celebrate 300 years of religious liberty. It is a pleasure to come into the synagogue to worship, for the edifice is a sister of Trinity Church. They were built about the same time. The people who founded them were prompted by the same spirit. I am worried over what is going on in this country today. From some source is coming propaganda against the Jews. Have the Jews injured any community in which they have flourished? No! They have helped in music, in literature and philosophy. If the Jew is determined and persists in his line of endeavor it is not because he is any different than any other nationality or creed. The Jewish people have kept faith and believe in God. The Jew today has a great deal to teach the Gentile. Let us pray that the spirit of today will long continue.[6]

Mr. Gainer pointed out in part:

> We should rejoice in the fact that we were among the pioneers that gave to the nation its basic principle of government, religious and civil liberty as founded in Rhode Island by Roger Williams and John Clarke. We must not be satisfied to sit idly by and boast about the glory of our ancestors. We have a right to be proud of our heritage, but we must be prepared to defend it.[7]

A Monument of Freedom

In addition to expressing their gratitude with praises and prayer, the Jews of Newport decided to erect and dedicate a monument of freedom that should go down to posterity as an eternal memorial of "the Declaration of Religious and Civil Liberty in the Colony of Rhode Island." [8]

On August 20, 1939, the Jews of Newport dedicated this monument to religious liberty on the *Touro Synagogue* grounds. It was presented to the city as a token of sincere appreciation for its hospitality extended to all weary, wandering and tired souls and in gratitude for its contribution to three centuries of freedom and to the preservation of the synagogue.

The monument, consisting of a simple three-sided pyramid seven feet high, was erected of Rhode Island fieldstone. On it was placed a bronze tablet inscribed with the seal which the people of Newport and Portsmouth adopted in 1640, and with a quotation from the Rhode Island Charter of 1663:

> That noe person within the sayd colonye, at any time hereafter shall bee any wise molested, punished, disquieted, or called in question, for any difference in opinion in matters of religion which doe not actually disturb the civill peace of our sayd colonye; but that all and everye person and persons may, from tyme to tyme, and at all tymes hereafter, freelye and fullye have and enjoye his and theire owne judgments and consciences, in matters of religious concernments.[9]

The erection of the monument of religious liberty on the grounds of the *Touro Synagogue* and its presentation to the City of Newport were hailed by the local and national press as the greatest contribution of any group to the city's Tercentenary and to the ideals of American democracy and concept of freedom. It was not without significance that at a time when a large part of the world was clothed in darkness of hatred, persecution, and massacre, and the world was on the brink of war and blood shed, that in a small old town in America, Jew, Catholic, and Protestant should gather in brotherhood and understanding to dedicate a monument to religious liberty and freedom.

The dedication celebration evoked awe for the significance of the occasion. Outstanding national dignitaries were present. Radio carried the solemn exercises to every part of the country where millions were enabled to share in the glory of God and high ideals of man. The exercises were opened with prayers by Dr. Morris A. Gutstein, the rabbi of the *Touro Synagogue* at the time, and closed with prayers by Dr. David de Sola Pool. Judge Max Levy, chairman of the arrangements committee and presiding officer of the dedication ceremonies read the messages from President Franklin Delano Roosevelt, Governor Herbert Lehman and Mayor F. H. LaGuardia of New York, commending the occasion and lauding the long history of the synagogue. An outstanding feature of the exercise was the re-enactment of George Washington's visit to Newport, in 1790, when the first president of the United States exchanged addresses with Moses Seixas, the then warden of the historic synagogue. The original addresses were read by W. Selden Washington, a great-great-great grandnephew of the first president and by Edward Jonas Philips direct descendant of Moses Seixas. During the exercise the monument was unveiled by Governor William Vanderbilt and Dr. Gutstein.

In unveiling the monument the governor summed up eloquently the significance of the occasion:

> This Tercentenary observation is of paramount importance and of great meaning at this time particularly. Exactly three hundred years ago when William Coddington and John Clarke and a handful of pilgrim followers of Roger Williams settled in the southern tip of Aquidneck Island, in what is now the city of Newport, they were

seeking a freedom that was then unknown either in the Old World or in any colony in the New World. These men fled the oppression of the Old World and in turn fled the Puritan persecution of the Massachusetts Bay Colony because they were determined that in their new home all men should be able to worship as their consciences dictated, every one in the name of his God. Freedom of conscience as related to religious liberty was born here when in 1641 the first law granting complete religious and civil liberty ever embodied in the legislation of any civilized state was enacted.   ,

It is fitting in these times that this monument commemorating the wisdom and tolerance of the founding fathers should be presented to this city by the Hebrew Congregation.

Newporters and Rhode Islanders of every faith and creed have distinguished themselves in many varied fields of endeavor and have contributed much to the upbuilding of this city, this State and this Nation. May they continue in generations to come and may the record of the past be a constant inspiration for the future. Let us all remember the three things for which our forebearers stood and which made them great - Independence, Courage, Tolerance.[10]

The principal speaker at the dedication ceremonies was United States Senator David I. Walsh of Massachusetts. Said Senator Walsh:

Happily we are not threatened with the loss of religious freedom in America, but candor compels us to admit that we are suffering from a substantial loss of religion.

The message which you have invited me to bring to you today cannot be more appropriately introduced than by directing your attention to the quotation from the Charter of King Charles in 1663 and inscribed on this monument. There is another inscription however, that is on one of the public buildings in the city of Washington that I desire to use for my text today. It contains a sentiment that applies both to nations and to men - *God made us neighbors, Let justice make us friends.*

If every American Protestant, American Catholic and American Jew could live this sentiment, they would not only give public manifestation of the sincerity of their religious belief, but we would indeed all really live in the sunlight of American Liberty. The progress of mankind through the centuries has given to us many priceless heritages. Outstanding among them all is what we call Religious Liberty. Religious Liberty in America means that the state guarantees to every individual freedom of conscience; that intermeddling by the civil authority with religious institutions, doctrines, discplines or exercises is absolutely forbidden.

Each man naturally feels strongly about the rightfulness of his own faith; and in proportion to how he feels, so he must think that other men with other faiths are wrong. This was one of the defects in the Puritans' philosophy, for though deeply religious, yet, they were unwilling to recognize the religious rights of others.

To a degree, we are witnessing today the spirit of 300 years ago, which was a persecuting spirit. It was then abroad in many parts of the world. Today it is abroad in many parts of the world with even greater intensity than 300 years ago. Today it is called by a different name but racial discrimination is just as foreign to the spirit of religious liberty as is religious persecution.

Religious liberty is the outgrowth of the long struggle of mankind with religious persecutions. It is the outstanding victory for human dignity and human liberty won by the common man after the centuries he and his children had groaned under a contrary concept of state's right and duty. And no group of human beings has borne that yoke longer and with more cruelty than the Jew.[11]

Among the other speakers, Dr. James P. Adams, Vice-president of Brown University described the occassion as the unveiling of a monument to the cornerstone of American democracy. Then he continued:

It is a fundamental tenet of our academic faith. What other spot in the world except here where Roger Williams bequeathed this great tradition to us could we gather with more pride and understanding? It is significant that religion is not on the defensive in the United States. Freedom of conscience is not a political concern, but is a moral right.[12]

Isadore S. Worth, National Commander of the Jewish War Veterans of America commented:

Newport is more than a beautiful and historic city. It is a living reminder of the most cherished heritage of the American people - the heritage of democratic progress based on Unity. It is our answer to those subversive forces of Communism and Fascism which dare to spread the seeds of hatred and dis-unity in a land which has grown great through the inner unity of all Americans - a brotherhood springing from mutual respect for the highest aspirations of the human spirit, whether they be expressed in temple, church or meeting house.[13]

"Aaron Lopez and Judah Touro"

To add a literary contribution to Newport's Tercentenary, Rabbi Morris A. Gutstein chose to publish and dedicate to the City of Newport two biographies: one of a refugee - Aaron Lopez - and one of the son of a refugee - Judah Touro.[14] Both of these personalities epitomize the contribution of Jewry to America. Aaron Lopez, "the merchant prince of Colonial Newport" symbolizes free enterprise and commerce which have advanced our country economically. Judah Touro epitomizes the spirit of Jewish charity and philanthropy, as it extends to all peoples of all creeds and cultural and racial backgrounds. Both Aaron Lopez and Judah Touro, were closely associated with Newport. It was therefore most appropriate to present this book formally to the city as part of its Tercentenary observance.

The presentation of the book to the city took place Tuesday, October 31st, 1939. It was thus described in the press:

> With ceremonies that included addresses that recalled the contribution of the Jewish people to Newport's history, Rabbi Morris A. Gutstein's book "Aaron Lopez and Judah Touro - a Refugee and the Son of a Refugee" dedicated to the city on its Tercentenary, was presented to Mayor Henry S. Wheeler, in behalf of the city, Tuesday evening at the *Jewish Community Center.*
>
> Judge Robert M. Dannin made the presentation. Mayor Wheeler, in accepting, told of the part played by the Jews in the city's history. Other addresses were made by Judge Mortimer A. Sullivan of the Superior Court, Rabbi Israel M. Goldman of Temple Emanuel, Providence. A. L. Greenberg, chairman of the publication committee, was master of ceremonies.[15]

In accepting the book Mayor Wheeler said:

> It is a privilege and an honor to accept this book, "Aaron Lopez and Judah Touro, a Refugee and Son of a Refugee," on behalf of the City of Newport in this our Tercentennial year.
>
> Much has been said this year, of the part played by the Jews in the history of our city. As if anticipating this anniversary, Dr. Gutstein contributed to the record of Newport his "Story of the Jews in Newport." Now he gives us the story of two individuals among these people and of their outstanding careers and their part in our city's history.

It is fitting that their story should be written at this particular time when other members of their faith abroad are experiencing the same suffering as the Jews of Spain and Portugal were forced to endure, two and three centuries ago.

Both names, Aaron Lopez and Judah Touro, should long remain in the hearts of the citizens of Newport.[16]

Judge Sullivan in his address paid his respects to the early founders of the Jewish colony. He then continued:

Newport held out a welcoming hand to the refugees of old. Our country today should emulate this example and open its doors to all refugees. The book should be sent to every library in the country, that people may know of the Jews of Newport, and of the message of freedom and opportunity.[17]

Rabbi Goldman of Providence commended highly the warm-hearted address of Judge Sullivan. "It was an address that should have been heard by all," said Rabbi Goldman, and he added that he was anxious for television for he would like to have all see as well as hear a Jewish judge presenting a book by a Jew to a leader of an American city who is of Protestant faith and a Catholic judge deliver the keynote address.[18]

Equality Versus Toleration

Barely a year had passed, and the one hundred and fiftieth year of the visit to Newport by George Washington in 1790, and the exchange of the addresses between the first president of our country and the "Hebrew Congregation in Newport" came around. This certainly was an occasion for celebration. No other group or organization, except the Jewish community and the *Touro Synagogue* of Newport and the *Message of Israel* radio program took cognizance of this momentous historic event.[19]

On August 17, 1940, the exact anniversary date of the exchange of the addresses, the *Message of Israel* national radio broadcast devoted its entire program to the George Washington address and to the fascinating story of the pioneering days of the Jew in Colonial America.

Rabbi Jonah B. Wise of the Central Synagogue of New York, from where the broadcast emanated, introduced the program by stating:

> The "Message of Israel" is devoted to America, Truth and Faith. These three ideas are now the pillars of the house sheltering humanity in the storm raging over the world. We put America first because it is chief amongst all the treasures of our world of yesterday, of today, and of tomorrow. I cannot foresee tomorrow but I do know it will not be a fit place for human dwelling unless there is in it a free America. I do see dimly today. There is here and now a need for America. There is a need for an America guided by truth and sustained by faith. The "Message of Israel" is consecrated to the faith of Israel and the truth about Israel and about America. There is today just because of raido, airplane, and other messengers, faster than Mercury, a power to the liar unparallelled in human experience. Truth travels more slowly. It often has not the wealth to command the modern miracles of communication and not the power to command the devilish ingenuity and mendacity of the propaganda forces of the new tyrannies. Liars need propagandists. Truth needs only honorable men. Once the world rises to the point where it knows the truth about Israel, the dawn of redemption for all is just over the horizon. One who is a living example of the valiant man armed with truth is George Washington. To speak of him today in connection with the leering, brutal conquerors of Europe is an association too foul to contemplate. Therefore we place him here tonight alone without company like a lighted alabaster statue before a black curtain. Tonight I want you to see him as he visits the house of prayer of the Jews in Newport, Rhode Island. It was 150 years ago. That house still stands and is used for worship by the Jews. George Washington is, for us, alive in the spirit, a worshipper with all of us at every shrine dedicated to truth, faith and liberty.[20]

After this introduction and the liturgical music, Dr. Gutstein presented a succinct resumé of the contribution of the Jewish people to Colonial America and to the American Revolutionary cause, and to the establishment of the republic. He went on to say:

> In the house of God it is not to military heroism or to victory of arms that we sing praises, but rather do we exalt the spirit of man as it manifests itself in all children of God, particularly in the chosen leaders who by their lives and actions proved that the world

can be a paradise if man will desire it to be so. It is of George Washington the man who has become a symbol of democracy, a champion of the concept of religious liberty, and the forebearer of the American spirit of the absolute equality of man, that we speak here.

The great contribution of George Washington to democracy is contained in his address to the Hebrew Congregaiton in Newport in which he states: "The citizens of the United States of America have a right to applaud themselves for having given to mankind examples of an enlarged and liberal policy; a policy worthy of imitation. All possess alike liberty of conscience and immunities of citizenship. It is now no more that toleration is spoken of as if it was by the indulgence of one class of people that another enjoyed the exercise of their inherent natural rights. For happily the Government of the United States, which gives to bigotry no sanction, to persecution no assistance, requires only that they who live under its protection, should demean themselves as good citizens, in giving it on all occasions their effectual support."

In these words, George Washington distinguished between two types of liberty: one, mere *Toleration*, another, real *Equality*.

Toleration may be defined as a more or less grudging permission of that which is not wholly approved. Webster gives one definition of "Tolerance" as: "the endurance of the presence or actions of objectionable persons, or of the expressions of offensive opinions."

Toleration is often liberty granted by one class of people to another which it considers weaker, inferior, wrongminded or different.

Equality, on the other hand, recognizes neither superior nor inferior. It is not a privilege granted by one class of people to another. It is the basis of the liberty enjoyed by all alike through common recognition of fundamental human rights. Equality is based on that human brotherhood, expressed by the prophet Malachi in his immortal words:

> *Have we not all One Father?*
> *Has not One God created us?*

The people of America in Colonial days had achieved in some respect religious liberty and freedom. However, with the exception of Rhode Island, where man's conscience concerned only himself and his God, and not at all the temporal powers to which as a citizen he is subject, religious liberty had not advanced beyond the concept of toleration.

It was this spirit and concept of liberty as founded on absolute equality of man, the fountainhead of our democracy in America, of which George Washington spoke to the Jews of Newport.

Today, a century and a half after this concept was expressed by the first president of the United States of America, people are no longer whipped in the streets of Boston because of being Baptists, nor hanged because of being Quakers. Catholics are not banished from one state or another, nor are Jews deprived of the full rights of citizenship. Yet, the fine grace of equality, conceived by Washington, liberty, as a modern preacher puts it, "with its love of free field and fair play for divergent ideas," liberty with its willingness to include in work and fellowhip all men of good will, irrespective of race, color or creed, liberty in the sense of equality, is still a lofty ideal not completely achieved.

The concept of equality as laid down by the Bible, taught by the sages, and proclaimed by the founding fathers of our country and our democracy is distinct from regimented uniformity. It does not intend that any give up their beliefs, practices and fundamental culture. The equality they conceived and we seek is a common effort to bring about mutual understanding and a frank recognition that each group in any commonwealth, as a modern writer puts it: "may and should develop the ideals and culture best fitted for itself, and that having done so, it can join with other groups to bring about a progressively better and finer country, with a truly great civilization." That is democracy based on the true spirit of equality as conceived by Washington, where everyone pursues his own way towards a common goal, the good for all.

All mankind is embarked on the ship of life in the sea of human civilization. Here and there mankind is menaced by surging waves and raging billows which hamper the progress of the ship of life. But the world and human nature are essentially good and progressive. There are instances at present, even as there have been at all times, of bigotry and persecution, the result of some psychosis of superiority and inequality. There have been periods in human history, even as today, when some groups of people "run amok." But the entire world is not running amok. Just as in the sky there occur clouds which obscure the blue and darken the light of the horizon, but which in due time pass away, so too, the wickedness of the earth shall pass away and the ship of life on the sea of human civilization shall ride on serenely and calmly.[21]

Sunday afternoon, August 18th, a special anniversary program commemorating the one hundred and fiftieth anniversary of George Washington's address took place at the *Touro Synagogue,* under the chairmanship of Albert L. Greenberg. Professor

Carl Bridenbaugh of Brown University and Dr. David de Sola Pool were the principal speakers.

Professor Bridenbaugh devoted his scholarly address to the architecture of the *Touro Synagogue* and to its architect and designer Peter Harrison. He traced the biography of the architect and then pointed out that Harrison anticipated American Classicism in architecture: "Thomas Jefferson, philosophial radical founded it. This synagogue therefore finds itself in the vanguard of the best traditions in American architecture." [22]

Professor Bridenbaugh alluded to the other buildings and architectural styles which Harrison designed, among them King's Chapel in Boston. Speaking about the Ark of the *Touro Synagogue,* he stated:

> When he came to the Ark he found himself in a genuine predicament. No such thing had ever been designed either for a Christian church or for a pagan temple. Here his imagination rose to the occasion and he achieved a magnificent solution by adapting for the lower part, the Ark proper, a design for a Tuscan altarpiece that he had previosuly used for the altar of King's Chapel and which is found in Batty Langley's *Treasury of Designs;* above it he placed an ornamental frame which appears to be a fusion of one of Kent's drawings with another taken from the *Designs of Inigo Jones and Others* by Isaac Ware. The finished design, however, was substantially modeled by his own notions of what the Ark ought to be.[23]

Professor Bridenbaugh concluded:

> The Jews and the Christians lived together in the olden days in complete harmony. Harrison, an Episcopalian, building a Jewish synagogue which is a model of classic Colonial architecture. The Ark of the synagogue—The Holy of Holies—following a Tuscan altarpiece used for King's Chapel, and a Christian minister—Dr. Ezra Stiles—attending the dedication of the synagogue and giving it the best description, are only a few historic examples of this good will among all creeds that we should learn to emulate.[24]

Dr. Pool interpreted the broad principles set up by George Washington, stating that "spiritual and religious liberties are rights rather than favors, now violated in some parts of the world, but continued in this country which has become a haven for the oppressed." He then continued:

Long before the time of George Washington, Spinoza had asked "what policy more self-destructive can any nation follow than to regard as public enemies men who have committed no crime or wickedness save that of freely exercising their intelligence," and we may add, save that of freely exercising their conscience. Yet this danger existed a century and a half ago in this land, notwithstanding the strong sectarian differences in the religious denominationalism of the thirteen states. Against this danger, George Washington took a firm, determined and consistent stand. Churchman though he was, he could not understand a concept of national liberty which gave physical freedom without spiritual freedom. He declared: "The cause of American liberty is the cause of every virtuous American citizen, whatever be his religion or descent." He who had led the fight for liberty understood the words of Leviticus cast on the Liberty Bell, "proclaim liberty throughout the land to all the inhabitants thereof" as meaning freedom of conscience as well as political freedom.

In the eyes of George Washington, this complete spiritual as well as civic liberty had to be not a grudged or a gracious concession, but a right. It was not to be toleration exercised by a privileged majority, it was to be religious equality. Again and again he expressed himself in this vein, as when he wrote to the *United Baptist Churches*: "Every man conducting himself as a good citizen and being accountable to God alone for his religious opinion ought to be protected in worshipping the Deity according to the dictates of his own conscience." Indeed, as he wrote to the Catholics, "As mankind become more liberal, they will be more apt to allow that all those who conduct themselves as worthy members of the community are equally entitled to the protection of civil government."

As the President of the Constitutional Convention, Washington labored to translate these broad, and what were then novel and revolutionary, sentiments into constitutional principles. His attention was forcibly drawn to this issue by Jonas Phillips, a leading member of *Congregation Shearith Israel*. In a memorial presented to Washington as President of that Constitutional Convention, Jonas Phillips asked that there should be no religious discrimination under the federal constitution which was being drafted: "Then the Israelites will think themselves happy to live under a government where all Religious Societys are on an Equal footing," and he added with prophetic insight: "I solicit this favor for myself, my children and posterity, and for the benefit of all the Israelites through the 13 United States of America."

In the result, in the first federal constitution adopted in 1787 these classic words were built into the foundation principles of this

Unveiling of Monument to Religious Freedom on the grounds of
the Touro Synagogue by Governor Vanderbilt and Rabbi Gutstein, 1936

Unveiling of Bronze Tablet erected by U.S. Department of
Interior designating Touro Synagogue as a National Historic Site

republic: "No religious test shall ever be required as a qualification to any office or public trust under the United States."

Yet this did not prove to be a sufficient safeguard. For conscientious observers of the seventh day Sabbath were still fined and imprisoned for working on Sunday. When this fact was brought to the attention of George Washington, he wrote: "If I had had the least idea of any difficulty resulting from the Constitution adopted by the Convention of which I had the honor to be President when it was formed, so as to endanger the rights of any religious denomination, then I never should have attached my name to that instrument. If I had any idea that the general government was so administered that liberty of conscience was endangered, I pray you be assured that no man would be more willing than myself to revise and alter that part of it so as to avoid religious persecution."

These soothing words were not the suave insincerity of a professional politician, but the sincere conviction of an honest man. Washington encouraged James Madison to draw up the Bill of Rights amending the Constitution, containing the words: "Congress shall make no law respecting an establishment of religion or prohibiting the free exercise thereof."

Washington went still further, when at his urging there was included in the treaty with Tripoli, the statement that: "The government of the United States of America is in no sense founded on the Christian religion. The United States is not a Christian nation any more than it is a Jewish or a Mohammedan nation."

Washington himself took more than one occasion to give public and eloquent demonstration of his own utter freedom from religious prejudice, and his convictions that in this new America all religions must stand on a footing of equality. This was demonstrated when at his inauguration as first President of the United States the whole clergy of New York, including as we recall with pride, Gershom Mendes Seixas, the Minister of the *Congregation Shearith Israel* at the time, took official part in the parade and epoch making ceremonies.[25]

A National Shrine

Even as the Jews of Newport expressed their gratitude to the ideals of America with special Tercentenary services, a monument to religious liberty, a book on a refugee and a son of a refugee who enriched America, and a commemoration of George Washington's address, the United States expressed its gratitude to the Jews of America by making the *Touro Synagogue* in Newport a *National Historic Site,* making it thus the first and only Jewish historic shrine in the country. This came about by resolution of the *United States Department of Interior* in 1946, in accordance with an act passed in 1935, which stipulated: "that it is a national policy to preserve for public use historic sites, buildings and objects of national significance for the inspiration and benefit of the people of the United States." Only three other houses of worship have been thus designated: *San Jose Mission,* near San Antonio, Texas, in 1941; *Gloria Dei (Old Swede's) Church* in Philadelphia, in 1942; and *Saint Paul's Church,* in Eastchester, New York, in 1943. *San Jose* is Roman Catholic, *Gloria Dei* was originally Lutheran but is now Protestant Episcopal and *Saint Paul's* is also Protestant Episcopal. Thus Catholic, Protestant and Jew are linked historically with the beginnings of the ideal of religious liberty in this country. The *Gloria Dei* church goes back to 1700; the *San Jose Mission* was established in 1720; the *Saint Paul's Church* dates from 1774.[26]

Because the *Congregation Shearith Israel* of New York is the legal owner and trustee of Newport's *Touro Synagogue,* and the *Congregation Jeshuat Israel* is the lessee of the building, the *United States Department of the Interior* had to enter into an agreement with both congregations. The agreement points out the reason why the *Touro Synagogue* was designated a *National Historic Site* under the provision of the Act of Congress:

WHEREAS, the historic Touro Synagogue building, Newport, Rhode Island, is a splendid example of the architectural genius of Peter Harrison, one of the pre-eminent architects of the colonial period of American History; and,

WHEREAS, the Advisory Board on National Parks, Historic Sites, Buildings, and Monuments has declared that the historic Touro Synagogue, Newport, Rhode Island is of national historical significance; and,

WHEREAS, the Shearith Israel Trustees, the owners of the Touro Synagogue, and the Congregation Jeshuat Israel, the lessee of the Synagogue building and conducting worship therein desire to promote the designation of the said Touro Synagogue as a national historic site and to preserve, protect and maintain it in perpetuity for all necessary and desirable public and religious purposes, for the inspiration and benefit of the people of the United States and particularly to continue to foster on the part of the people of the Nation through visits to this shrine, a sincere devotion to the United States and to the principles of religious freedom for which it stands, and for the perpetuation of this country's architectural and cultural heritage; and,

WHEREAS, it is the desire of the Secretary to cooperate with the Shearith Israel Trustees and with the Congregation Jeshuat Israel, in preserving the integrity of the Touro Synagogue for the benefit and inspiration of the people of the United States:

NOW THEREFORE, in consideration of the foregoing and pursuant to the authority contained in the Act of Congress approved August 21, 1935 (49 Stat. 666), entitled "An Act to provide for the preservation of historic American buildings, objects, and antiquities of national significance and for other purposes," the said parties have covenanted and agreed and by these presents do covenant and agree to and with each other in consideration of the mutual promises expressed as follows:

The Shearith Israel Trustees and Congregation Jeshuat Israel agree for themselves, their respective successors and assigns:

a) That they will preserve, protect, maintain, and, when necessary, restore, so far as lies within their power, the Touro Synagogue, Newport, Rhode Island, and the grounds immediately about the Synagogue building . . .

b) That they will not erect, or permit to be erected, any building or buildings on any portion of the grounds mentioned above . . . without prior approval in writing by the Secretary.

c) That they will consult with the National Park Service before permitting the erection or replacement of any monument, marker, tablet or other memorial in or upon the said Touro Synagogue or any portion of the grounds herein referred to, designated by the Secretary as part of the national historic site.

d) That no structural alterations to said Touro Synagogue, and no substantial repairs affecting the appearance thereof shall be undertaken by them until the plans therefor have been submitted to, and approved in writing by, the Secretary.

e) That they will consult with the National Park Service regarding the decoration and furnishing of the interior of the building.

f) That the public shall be admitted to all parts of the said Touro Synagogue, excepting such rooms or space as may be reserved for the keeping of religious vestments, vessels, monies, and historical or valuable personal properties, at all reasonable times, so far as consistent with the preservation of the Synagogue and the

maintenance of divine services in accordance with the ritual, rights
and customs of the Orthodox Spanish and Portuguese Jews as practiced and observed in the Synagogue of said *Congregation Shearith
Israel*.[27]

Although the synagogue was designated as a *National Historic Site* in 1946, the dedication did not take place until the
summer of 1947. The delay was due to the problem involved
in the arrangements. Originally President Harry S. Truman was
expected to be the keynote speaker at the dedication. The program
and date of the dedication were planned to fit the schedule of the
president. It developed, however, that pressing matters of the
government made it impossible for the president to attend at any
time. When the date was finally set, Congressman Joseph W.
Martin, Jr. of Massachusetts, Speaker of the House of Representatives, was invited to be the keynote speaker. President Truman
sent a letter of congratulation addressed to the president of
Touro Synagogue saying:

Dear Dr. Friedman:
    I am happy to congratulate Congregation Jeshuat Israel and the
community of Newport, Rhode Island, on the setting apart of the
Touro Synagogue as a national shrine. It is fortunate that the
venerable fabric of the Synagogue opened on December 2, 1763, a
century after the founding of the Congregation, is still in use and
admired by all lovers of good architecture.
    The setting apart of this historic shrine as a national monument
is symbolic of our tradition of freedom which has inspired men and
women of every creed, race and ancestry to contribute their highest
gifts to the development of our national culture. I trust through
long centuries to come that the spirit of good will and tolerance
will ever dominate the hearts and minds of the American people.
                                Very sincerely yours,
                                (Signed) Harry S. Truman

The dedication celebration lasted three days, from Friday,
August 29th through Sunday the 31st. It commenced with the
Sabbath Eve Service conducted by Dr. Louis C. Gerstein, rabbi
of *Congregation Shearith Israel* in New York. Dr. Israel M.
Goldman, who, at that time, was president of the Rabbinical
Assembly of America, preached the sermon. In his sermon, Dr.

Goldman spoke of the spiritual influence of the Touro Synagogue on all American Jewry.

At the Oneg Shabbat that followed the service, Mrs. David de Sola Pool spoke on the theme "A Crucible of Faith - The Story of the Marranos." This was in keeping with the historic fact that former Marranos were the founders of the original *Congregation Yeshuat Israel* and the builders of the synagogue.

Saturday morning, Dr. Morris A. Gustein, former rabbi of the *Touro Synagogue,* delivered an address on the historic significance of the *Touro Synagogue* to American Judaism and Jewry.

Saturday evening the Honorable John H. Greene, Jr., president of the *Sons of the Revolution in Rhode Island,* addressed the community at a special gathering in the synagogue. He spoke on the "Contribution of the Jews of the Past to the Development of Newport." This was followed by an address by Dr. David de Sola Pool on the "History of the Jews of Newport - 1850-1890."[28]

The Dedicatory Exercises took place Sunday, August 31st. A distinguished assembly of "national, state and local religious and lay figures" filled the beautiful interior of the oldest Jewish house of worship in the United States and overflowed to the lawn outside, as the three-day program of solemn dedication reached its climax.

The keynote address was then given by the Honorable Joseph W. Martin, Jr. In his address Speaker Martin described America as "almost the last haven of liberty and almost the last abode of freedom and justice." He then continued:

> Symbolic of our deep-rooted tradition of religious freedom, this long-revered house of worship now testifies to the spirit of good will and brotherhood that prevails among Americans of every faith.
>
> We have been able to attain here in America the greatest spiritual and cultural progress, the greatest degree of religious and political liberty, the greatest amount of luxuries, the highest wages, and the finest working conditions, and the best education system in the world.
>
> Free government, personal liberty, the progress of civilization, hang in the balance today, and America must lead the way back to peace if the nations of the world are to find peace.

America stands today as the bulwark of liberty and freedom. We stand as a living torch of hope, as a living beacon of freedom for liberty loving peoples all over the earth. Our republican form of government will not long endure if intolerance makes substantial headway.

Congressman Martin concluded:

This building has seen the ebb and flow of American history.

Today it calls us to keep the faith! For as long as Protestants, Catholics and Jews worship side by side in peace, as long as we work together in harmony, differences subordinated in common devotion to our ideals - so long will our land be strong and happy within - and worthy of leading the other nations in the noble search for a better world for all mankind.

Speakers in addition to Congressman Martin were Senator Theodore Francis Green; His Excellency, John O. Pastore, Governor of Rhode Island; the Right Reverend Granville Gaylord Bennett, Episcopal Bishop of the Diocese of Rhode Island; Carl Van Doren, noted American historian; and Dr. Francis S. Rolands, regional director of the *National Park Service, Department of the Interior.*

Alderman John J. Dannin brought the city's greetings in behalf of Mayor Edward G. Gladding; Henry S. Hendricks, president of *Congregation Shearith Israel,* spoke for his congregation; and Dr. Bernard C. Friedman, president of the *Congregation Jeshuat Israel,* for the *Touro Synagogue* congregation. Dr. Samuel Adelson, general chairman of the dedication committee, presided over the Dedicatory Exercises.[29]

Part of the Dedicatory Exercises was the unveiling of a tablet on the southern wall of the Synagogue by Dr. Francis S. Ronalds:

NATIONAL HISTORIC SITE
TOURO   SYNAGOGUE
of
JESHUAT ISRAEL CONGREGATION
Founded 1658

This oldest synagogue building in the United States was designed by Peter Harrison. Ground was broken August 1, 1759. It was dedicated on December 2, 1763. Here 1781-84 the Rhode Island

General Assembly met, and during Washington's visit to Newport in 1781, a town meeting was held here. The State Supreme Court held sessions here at that period. The building was reopened for religious services on August 2, 1850.[30] In 1790[31] George Washington wrote to this Congregation that . . . "Happily the government of the United States . . . gives to bigotry no sanction, to persecution no assistance."

National
Park Service
UNITED STATES   (Seal)
DEPARTMENT OF THE INTERIOR

Major Louis Ellis, a White House aide, and George Williams, of the Treasury Department, represented the United States government at the exercises.

The Dedicatory Exercises were broadcast over local and national radio stations. The dedication program concluded with a festival banquet in the evening, presided over by Mr. Julius Schaffer, secretary of the shrine dedication committee. Dr. F. S. Dannin, vice-chairman of the committee extended greetings on behalf of the community. The principal speaker was Judge Mortimer A. Sullivan of the *Superior Court of Rhode Island.*

By designating the *Touro Synagogue* as a *National Historic Site,* the United States of America has not only given recognition to the early Jewish pioneers and their contributions to the building of our republic, but also demonstrated that Catholic, Protestant and Jew even as they have fought and died together to win and to retain our democratic way of life, can live together in harmony and in peace, working hand in hand, and side by side in common devotion, for a better world, a better tomorrow and a better mankind.

The dedication of the *Touro Synagogue* as a national shrine demonstrates that the American belief in human rights, equality and opportunity is still vibrant.

The story of the three-hundred year old Jewish community of Newport, the one hundred and ninety-five year old historic synagogue, the Jewish shrine in America, not only forms one of the most fascinating chapters in the history of religious liberty in America but is a lesson in the immortality of man and the spirit of America. It illustrates what a poet once wrote:

> *Here where the savage roamed and fought;*
> *God sowed the seed of nobler thought;*
> *Here to the land we love to claim,*
> *The pioneers of freedom came;*
> *Here has been cradled all that's best,*
> *In every human mind and breast.*
> *For full four hundred years and more*
> *Our land has stretched her welcoming shore*
> *To weary feet from soils afar;*
> *Soul-shackled serf of kings and czar*
> *Have journeyed here and toiled and sung*
> *And talked of freedom to their young*
> *And God above has smiled to see*
> *This precious work of liberty.*[32]

APPENDIX

A Street, a Park and a Statue

It has been stated in the text that we cannot ascertain definitely when the historic *Colonial Sanctuary* in Newport became known as *Touro Synagogue*. It probably came about after the demise of Abraham Touro, when the endowment fund for the repair of the synagogue was established with the legacy for that purpose provided in Abraham Touro's will. While that fund was officially established as the "Abraham Touro Fund," it became known popularly as the *Touro Synagogue Fund*. The official municipal records of 1823 speak of the "Touro Jewish Synagogue." [1] Hence the name *Touro Synagogue*. Since the early part of the nineteenth century this name has thus come to be used for the historic synagogue. When the synagogue was reconsecrated in 1883, the name *Touro Synagogue* appears in the printed *Order of Service*. The stationery of the *Congregation Jeshuat Israel* in 1894, reads: *Touro Synagogue Chambers - Jeshuat Israel*.

1

The naming of the street on which the synagogue is located *Touro Street* did come about by resolution. The general impression prevails that the street was named *Touro* in honor of Reverend Isaac Touro or Judah Touro. Documentary evidence, however, reveals that the street's name was changed from "Griffin" to "Touro," in honor of Abraham Touro.

In his will Abraham Touro bequeathed:

> to the Municipal authority of the Town of Newport in Rhode Island, the sum of Five thousand dollars, in Special Trust and confidence, that they will appropriate the same in such manner they may judge best, for repairing and preserving the Street leading from the Burying Ground in said Town to the Main Street.

153

At a meeting of the *Municipal Council of the Town of Newport*, held at City Hall, on Monday, June 2, 1823, a communication was received from Titus Wells, informing "the Municipal Authority of the Town of Newport in the State of Rhode Island" of the bequest of Abraham Touro. Mr. Wells was the executor of the will, and he expressed confidence that the Council will accept the bequest and arrange for the execution of the benefactor's request.

Subsequent meetings of the *Town Council* continued to consider the bequest of Abraham Touro, resulting in the resolutions to accept the legacy, to deposit the five thousand dollars in the *New England Commercial Bank* and then to withdraw and invest the money "in such Bank Stock in the Town of Newport as . . . may prove most productive . . . and that said stock be known as the Touro fund, for repairing and preserving said Street, agreeably to the Intentions of the Donor." On April 17, 1824, the *Town Council* resolved that it become the trustees of this fund and proceed at once to repair the street. On July 20, 1824, the committee, appointed to repair the street, reported back to the *Council* as the "Trustees of Touro Street fund." On January 4, 1825, the minutes of the *Town Council* in recording the progress on the repair, refer to the street in parenthesis, "now called Touro Street." In appreciation of the munificence of Abraham Touro, the *Town Council* at a meeting on August 31, 1824, had passed a resolution:

> Whereas Abraham Touro a native of this town and late of Boston in the State of Massachusetts deceased, in his last will and testament devised to the Municipal Authority of this town a very ample fund, for the purpose of repairing and preserving the street leading from the Jews' burying ground to the Main Street. It is therefore voted and resolved in testimony and gratitude and esteem, for the memory of the said Abraham Touro, that the Street from Spring Street, Easterly (heretofore called Griffin Street), be hereafter known and called by the name of Touro Street.[2]

2

The naming of *Touro Park* also came about by resolution. In his last testament, Judah Touro willed:

> I give and bequeath to the City of Newport, in the State of Rhode Island, the sum of Ten thousand dollars, on condition that the said sum be expended in the purchase and improvement of the property in said City, known as the "Old Stone Mill," to be kep* as a public park or promenade ground.

The bequest was very graciously accepted by the municipal authorities, and the mayor was authorized to negotiate the purchase of the *Old Stone*

Mill and the grounds around it. On September 5, 1854, Mayor William C. Cozzens reported his success in purchasing the *Old Stone Mill,* and the land surrounding it, with the intention to convert it into a public park to be named *Touro Park* in honor of Judah Touro.

On that occasion the mayor expressed his sentiment in the following words:

> I congratulate our city upon this happy result, and trust that this beautiful site, with its hallowed associations, may be enjoyed by the citizens of Newport for ages to come; and the name, and I hope, the statue of the benevolent Israelite, by whose magnificent donation it has been principally achieved, may be forever associated with it.[3]

The mayor's wish to have the statue of Judah Touro in the park was never realized.

3

A movement to erect a monument to Judah Touro in the form of some kind of a statue began soon after the passing of the great philanthropist. On January 23, 1854, the City Council of New Orleans passed a resolution authorizing the erection of a suitable monument to Judah Touro somewhere in the city. An architect was consulted and engaged to present a plan. The architect's plan called for a statue of a group of heroic figures representing *charity.* It was to have been executed in bronze and was to take two years to make. However, this plan never materialized.[4]

In 1860, the idea to erect a monument to Judah Touro was revived by a special group that was organized under the name of *Touro Monument Association.* Important public officials joined the movement. The people of New Orleans were enthused about the project. The *Touro Monument Association* was sponsored primarily by the membership of the *Congregation Nefutzoth Yehudah* in New Orleans, which was usually referred to as the *Portuguese congregation.* Judah Touro had supported that congregation very liberally. In 1847 he purchased the *Protestant Episcopal Church* building on Bourbon and Canal Streets; spent a great deal of money to convert it into a synagogue; then presented it to the *Congregation Nefutzoth Yehudah* as his gift. Judah Touro also loaned the money to the congregation to purchase a cemetery.[5]

In appreciation of this and other benefactions, the people felt that Judah Touro merited recognition by having a public monument erected and dedicated in his honor. The plan called for some kind of a statue of Judah Touro. An appeal to the Jewish people to assist financially in this project and to make possible the erecting of the monument was sent out by Rabbi James K. Gutheim, the spiritual leader of the

Portuguese congregation. The plan was not just mere idle fancy. It was fully worked out and ready to have been executed were it not for a very interesting incident, in which the nineteenth century Jewish traveler (I. J.) Benjamin II played a rather important role. It is from Benjamin's two-volume travelogue *Three Years In America* 1859-1862,[6] published recently, in English translation, that we learn of this interesting incident.

During his travels in the United States, in April 1860, Mr. Benjamin visited New Orleans. A special organization *Benjamin Society* was organized to promote Benjamin's journeys "for the sake of increasing our knowledge of Jewish conditions in remote parts of the world." At a meeting of that society, on April 27th, the president of *Congregation Shaare Chesed,* among other things announced that "the *Portuguese congregation* had disclosed to him that they wished to set up a statue of Judah Touro to the lasting memory of the man who had been a benefactor of so many congregations." The statue of Judah Touro was to have been cast in bronze and set up in the outer court of the *Nefutzoth Yehudah* synagogue. Various other congregations in America were to be solicited for financial assistance to help in the implementation of this project. Upon hearing this, Mr. Benjamin asked for the privilege to speak, and he denounced completely the idea of a statue of Judah Touro as "unJewish" and as "clearly against the principles of our holy religion." [7]

Benjamin did not leave the matter rest with this. The next day he visited with Rabbi J. K. Gutheim to ascertain whether the plan was being earnestly considered, and was not just rumor. To his astonishment, Benjamin learned that Rabbi Gutheim was fully in accord with the plan of a Judah Touro monument and that he favored its implementation. Rabbi Gutheim was not concerned with the religious scruples against the idea at all and told Mr. Benjamin that he will proceed to see that "this statue will be set up." Upon this, Benjamin published his protest in the Anglo-Jewish publication *Cornerstone.* The protest caused great commotion among the Jews of New Orleans and throughout the country. As expected diverse opinions began to circulate. Interestingly enough Dr. Isaac M. Wise justified editorially in *The Israelite* Benjamin's position. Dr. David Einhorn, another spokesman for Reform Judaism, expressed his opposition to a statue. On the other hand the spokesmen for Orthodoxy were silent in the matter. Leeser in *The Occident,* and Isaacs in *The Jewish Messenger* at first made no comments at all, but only later upheld Benjamin's opinion. In view, however, of Benjamin's opinion, which has caught fire and soon became a national issue, the committee to set up the Judah Touro statue decided to submit the question to important European rabbinic authorities. They selected Rabbi Nathan M. Adler of London, Rabbi Samuel Hirsch of Frankfort-on-the-Main, Rabbi Solomon L. Rapaport of Prague, and Rabbi Zechariah Frankel of Breslau, to inquire of them whether the erection of a monument to Judah Touro in the form of a statue is permissible according to Jewish religious law and usage. All expressed their opinion against it, and the plan was disbanded.[8]

GLOSSARY

Ashkenazim — Jews residing elsewhere than in Spain and Portugal, more especially the Jews of Germany, Eastern and Central Europe and their descendants.

Ashkenazic — Applying to Ashkenazim.

Auto-da-fé — (Act of Faith) The solemn proclamation and subsequent execution of a judgment rendered by the Court of the Inquisition. Also the actual burning of the victims of the Inquisition in a public ceremony in the market place.

Banca — Bench, the seat in which the President of the Congregation sits. In the Synagogue in Newport it is the elevated seat adjacent to the northern wall.

Bar Mitzvah — (Son of Commandent) The ceremony or religious observance associated with the reaching of religious maturity of a Jewish boy of 13.

Beth Chayim — Literally *House of the Living*, or *Abode of Life*, the traditional Jewish designation of a Burial Ground.

Bikur Holim — (Visiting the Sick) Name of a charitable organization devoted to visiting the sick and general help to the needy.

Chacham — Ordained Rabbi, the Sephardic title of the Rabbi.

Chazan — Cantor or Reader of the Prayers at the Synagogue.

Gabay — Trustee.

God's acre — Cemetery.

Haham — (See Chacham).

Hazan — (See Chazan).

Haggadah — Order of Service used for the Seder.

Hechal — Ark in the Synagogue where the Scrolls of the Law are kept.

Holy Office — The Tribunal of the Inquisition in Spain and Portugal.

K. K. — Abbreviation of Kahal Kadosh.

Kakal Kadosh — Holy Congregation.

Kosher — "Suitable," "fit," Food fit to be eaten according to the Jewish ritual.

Matzo, (pl. Matzot) — Unleavened bread, eaten on Passover.

Mikveh — Ritual Bath.

Minhag Sephardim — The custom of the Spanish-Portuguese Jews in the Synagogue ritual.

Marranos — Jews of Spain and Portugal or their possessions, from the 15th century onward, who perforce lived outwardly as Catholics, while some secretly adhered to Judaism.

Mahamad — Standing committee or Board of Trustees.

Mitzvah (pl. Mitzvoth) — Commandment, good deed, religious duty.

Nedabah — A free will gift, also an alm or donation.

Parnas — President of the Congregation (Plural Parnasim).

Obtaining the Covenant — Used in context of letter of Aaron Lopez to Abraham I. Abrahams to mean circumcision.

Pessach (Passover) — The Festival celebrating the Exodus from Egypt.

Relapsi — Members of the church (especially Marranos) who have relapsed from the Catholic faith (by reverting to Judaism).

Rabbi — Literally, My Master, title of the Spiritual Leader of the Congregation; ordained person to decide on Jewish ritual law.

Rosasanah (Rosh Hashanah) — Jewish Religious New Year.

Seder — Home Service on the first two eves of Passover.

Shearith Israel — Remnant of Israel.

Schochet — One who slaughters cattle or fowl according to the ritual requirements of the Jewish law.

Semito — Sabbatical year, used by Stiles in the sense of 7 years in the interpretation of "Time, Times and a half."

Shovuoth — Pentecost, the Festival of Weeks, seven weeks after the second day of Passover.

Sephardim — Jews of Spain and Portugal or the Mediterranean area and their descendants.

Sephardic — Applying to the Jews of Spain and Portugal and their descendants.

Talmud Torah — Jewish Religious School.

Tebah — The Reading-desk in the Synagogue situated as a rule in the center of the Synagogue.

Tephilims - should be Tephilin — Phylacteries worn by male worshippers during morning services on weekdays.

Tishah B'Ab or (B'Av) — Ninth day of the Jewish month Av. Fast Day commemorating the destruction of the first and second Temple.

ARCHITECTURAL TERMS

Baroque — architectural style derived from the renaissance, characterized
   by giant columns, broken pediments, curved facades.
Belt-course — projecting horizontal band along the wall.
Palladian Window — tripartite window divided by columns with
   central partition arched.
Pediment — molded gable in classical architecture.
Portico — collonaded porch.
Reredos — ornamental screen in the back of an altar.

NOTES

Publication of the American Jewish Historical Society are abbreviated *PAJHS*.
The Story of the Jews of Newport by Morris A. Gutstein is referred to as *Gutstein*.

I

HOW CAME THEY HERE?

1. Historic Sites Act (49 Stat. 666) of the American Congress, adopted on August 21, 1935, authorizes the Federal government to enter into cooperate agreements with various bodies including "religious institutions" to accomplish desired historical conservation.
2. See *Jewish Advocate*, Boston, Tercentenary issue, January 27, 1955, p. 7
3. *Early Religious Leaders*: Newport Historical Society, p. 14.
4. Oscar S. Strauss, *Life of Roger Williams*, p. 178.
5. Edward Peterson, *History of Rhode Island and Newport in the Past*, p. 101. A quaint and almost cryptic document preserved in the archives of the Masonic Order is often cited as proof that the first settlement of Jews in Newport dates from the year 1658, when fifteen Jewish families of Spanish-Portuguese origin, in search for freedom, are said to have settled in the city. The document reads: "Ths ye (day and month obliterated) 165 (6 or 8, not certain which, as the place was stained or broken; the first three were plain) Wee mett att y House off Mordecai Campunall and affter Synagog Wee gave Abm Moses the degrees of Maconrie."
It is quoted in *The Jews and Masonry in the United States Before 1810* by Samuel Oppenheim, *PAJHS* 19:11 ff. A critical analysis of the quotation, and the proof of the authenticity of the manuscript, is presented by Oppenheim in the article. See also *Rhode Island Jewish Historical Notes*, vol. 2, No. 4, p. 216 ff. for an evaluation of this document. In *PAJHS* 27:416 the manuscript is quoted as follows: "On ye 2nd Tisri A.M. 5518 we assembled at ye

house of Mordecaiah Campanall and gave a degree to Abraham Moses."

There are a number of discrepancies between the two texts. Some inconsistencies in the latter quotation of the manuscript have been noticed by the Reverend Jacques Judah Lyons, when he copied the quotation from the original manuscript in the seventies of the last century. He noted: "How could this be done on the second day of Rosh Hashanah or was it on the night after the 2nd day, in which case it should have been dated 3rd of Tisri." In addition to this there is a more conspicuous discrepancy in the Lyons quotation between the date of the general calendar and the date of the Jewish calendar. 5518 which is the year according to the Jewish calendar given in the document does not correspond with 1658, but with 1757-1758, a hundred years later. But this is impossible in knowledge of the fact that in 1758 there was no Mordecai Campanall in Newport. Besides, the Masonic Lodge by that time was a fully developed institution in the city, having a regular meeting place and it did not meet in any private homes. Then we also possess the list of Jewish Masons who belonged to the Order in Newport, from the time the first Masonic Lodge was regularly constituted in the forties of the eighteenth century.

The only explanation of these discrepancies seems to be the fact that the manuscript when seen by Lyons was very much obliterated. The manuscript as quoted by Oppenheim comes from a reading of it in 1870 by N. Gould, who was the possessor of this valuable paper. At that time already, Gould noted in copying the document that part of the date was obliterated.

The Reverend J. J. Lyons copied the same manuscript in 1872. Although two years should not make much difference, yet, because of the age of the paper, it is quite plausible that by the time Lyons saw it, the reading was still more difficult, and the date was altogether obliterated. It may also be that Gould did not take the trouble to decipher the entire document especially the part containing the Hebrew date, which, the Reverend Jacques Lyons who was interested in it more from the point of view of Jewish history than masonry, did attempt to read it more completely. The error in the Hebrew date may simply be an error of Mr. Lyons' in copying or an attempt to render the obliterated date more fully.

The words "and affter Synagog," which do not appear in the Lyons' quotation, were probably altogether missing at the time he copied it.

However, whatever reasons there might be for the apparent differences in the reading of the original document concerning the first settlement of the Jews in Newport, all authorities on the subject agree that 1658 is the date the Jews first came to the shores of Rhode Island, as a group, and that they, immediately upon their arrival organized a congregation, which conducted its services in private houses for over a century until a synagogue was built.

6. See article "Inquisition" in the Jewish Encyclopedia, Vol. VI, p. 587 ff.

7. Paul Masserman and Max Baker, *The Jews Come to America,* p. 24 ff.

8. *PAJHS* 18:4.

9. Charles P. Daly, *The Settlement of the Jews in North America;* Jewish Encyclopedia, vol. IX, p. 294; Isaac Markens, *The Hebrews in America,* p. 33.

10. Cf. *Jewish Daily Forward, April* 4-5, 1939. In these issues of the Forward appeared two articles on *The First Celebration of Passover in America* by H. Lang. These articles were based on the book in Dutch published in 1939, by Gabriel Oderkerkesten. (The spelling of the name may not be correct inasmuch as I transliterated it from the Yiddish phonetically). The book was translated into English by a German-Jewish scholar Dr. Alfred Mannheimer. At the time of the writing of the articles in the Forward, the translation was in manuscript. The story of Habib is based on these articles.

11. According to this story, on arrival in Newport, Habib's relatives from Amsterdam met Dr. Rodrigues Malatesto, a Marrano, who had come to Newport from Maryland, in the interest of the Marranos. Dr. Malatesto joined the group at the celebration of the Seder. It was at this Seder, the author concludes, that the *Congregation Yeshuat Israel* was founded.

12. Peterson, supra, speaks of the Jews as coming from Holland. The author of Frankel's Wochenschrift, quoted in *PAJHS,* volume 6, by Max J. Kohler, claims that they came from Brazil. He bases his conclusion on the similarity between the name Campanall and Campanelli, who was one of the Jews who went to Brazil together with Rabbi Aboab in 1642, and lived there until the Portuguese conquered Brazil. Mordecai Campanal is said to have been among the fifteen families who came to Newport in 1658. (Cf. *PAJHS* 2:99). In view of the fact that a contingent of Spanish-Portuguese Jews did come to North America from Brazil, after the Portuguese conquest of 1654, the theory of the author in the Wochenschrift sounds plausible.

However, it may well be that the first permanent Jewish settlers in Newport, to which the quotation in Peterson's History refers, came from Barbados. This is possible, for a number of reasons.

First, we know, that Newport merchants were trading with Barbados at a very early period. And it might be, that because of this trade relationship, some Jews, upon hearing about the religious toleration in Rhode Island, decided to come here. Secondly, in a "List of Jews made Denizens in the Reign of Charles II and James II, 1661-1687," we find the name of "Moses Israel Pachoe," which was suggested to be amended to Pacheco, and who may be identical with Moses Pacheco, who together with Mordecai Campanall is associated with the purchase of the Burial Ground in Newport in 1677. We also find, other members of the Pacheco family in Barbados in 1680. (Cf. *PAJHS* 20:109 ff. and 1:105 ff.)

Dr. Pool was kind enough to call the writer's attention to the article "The Jewish Colonists in Barbados" by Wilfred S. Samuel, which is fully documented and definitely proves that the origin of the Jewish community of Newport was Barbados. Speaking about Simon Mendes who figures in 1684, in the resolution of the General Assembly giving the Jews rights to live in Rhode Island and assuring them full protection, Samuel says: "This SIMON MENDES was one of a little group of Speightstown Jews who early became identified with the congregation of Newport, Rhode Island - the oldest congregation of Jews in America. Its burial ground (to be celebrated two centuries later by Longfellow) had in February, 1677, been acquired by MORDECAI CAMPERNELL and one other Jew. A few months later Mordecai Campernell landed on the Island of Barbados and no doubt made his temporary home in St. Peter's Parish with DANIEL CAMPERNELL, Jew another of Lt. Col. Tidcom's militiamen. Mordecai Campernell was a Colonist of some experience who had formerly lived in Brazil, and he seems to have employed his time while visiting his kinsmen and friends on Barbados Island in persuading them of the far greater possibilities which were held out to settlers by Rhode Island. His colleague of the previous year in the purchase of the Newport burial ground has been MOSES ISRAEL PACHECO of Hamburg but also well known in Barbados, where he had settled at the Restoration, and whence he had successfully petitioned king Charles in the year 1662 for denization. Pachecho and Campernell's desire to secure recruits for the Jewish nucleus at Newport, R. I. was largely satisfied by Mordecai Campernell's mission to Barbados in 1678-79. On the 1st April, 1679, he shipped himself back to New England; ten days later he was followed by Abraham Burgos and Jacob Tinoco, both of Speights. On the 18th September Daniel Nasy (probably one of the Speightstown Fonsecas) sailed away in the ship HOPE for New England - Newport being perhaps his ultimate destination. Subsequently Simon Mendes with his wife, as well as the entire Campernell family left. On the 31st March 1685, - six years later - the Surveyor for Newport, R. I., commenced an action at law against the representative local Jews (in connexion with the burial ground) the eight defendants included the bearers of these familiar names: Abraham Burgos, Rachell, widow of Simon Mendes, Mordecai Campernell, David Campernell, Daniel Campernell and Abraham Campernell."

This seems to prove conclusively, that practically all the Jews who constituted the nucleus of the Jewish community, and who were later as a group brought to trial in 1685, came from Barbados. According to Samuel, the date of their settlement is not certain. But at all events they were in Newport already (at least some) before 1677. Samuel is not right in his statement that these Jews were brought to trial in connection with the burial ground. (See quotations from records of trial in text, also *PAJHS* vol. 19).

13. See note 5 of Chapter 4 infra, for a discussion of the name of the Newport congregation.
14. John S. Basset, *Short History of the United States,* p. 78.
15. The charter was interpreted to grant not only religious freedom but also freedom to trade.
16. *Copie of a Drought of the Town of Newport* by John Mumford, Jan. 3, 1712. Some have identified Griffin Street, which became Touro Street, as Jew's street, (cf. Broches, infra), probably because the synagogue is located on it. But this is an error.
17. Abraham P. Mendes, *The Jewish Cemetery,* Rhode Island Historical Magazine, October, 1885; *PAJHS* 27: 191; Cf. Gutstein, p. 295 ff.
18. The British began to pass Navigation Acts as early as 1651; Cf. Gutstein, p. 35; John S. Basset, supra.
19. *Records of the General Court of Trials,* 1671-1724, p. 72 ff.
20. John Russel Bartlett (editor) *Records of the Colony of Rhode Island and Providence Plantation,* vol. 3, p. 160.
21. Ibid.
22. *PAJHS* 10:142 ff; Joseph M. Corcos, *History of the Jews of Curaçao,* p. 7.
23. S. Broches, *Jews in New England I, Jewish Merchants in Colonial Rhode Island,* p. 7.
24. David and Tamar de Sola Pool, *An Old Faith in the New World,* p. 420.
25. George C. Mason, *Anals of the Redwood Library* p. 9.
26. Morris A. Gutstein, *Aaron Lopez and Judah Touro,* p. 11.
27. Broches supra; p. 9.

28. Ibid. p. 14.
29. Ibid. p. 11.
30. Ibid.
31. Ibid. p. 15 ff.
32. Bartlet, supra, vol. II, p. 138; vol. V, p. 375.
33. Gutstein, p. 53 ff.
34. Broches, supra, p. 14 ff.
35. Ibid. p. 21.
36. *PAJHS*, 27:445.
37. Broches, supra, p. 16.
38. *PAJHS*, 27:445.
39. Broches, supra, p. 13.
40. Ibid. p. 16.
41. Ibid. p. 8; Howard M. Chapin, *Rhode Island in Colonial Wars*, p. 87.
42. *Rhode Island Historical Magazine*, vol. IV, p. 58 ff.
The rules of the Jewish Men's Club are listed thus:

First. — The club is to be held every Wednesday evening during the winter season. The members to be nine in number; and by the majority of votes a chairman to be elected to serve one month only.

Second. — After one month, or four club nights, a new chairman to be elected in the manner aforesaid.

Third. — No person to be admitted as a member of said club without approbation of the members.

Fourth. — Each of the members shall have liberty to invite his friends to the club, well understood, one at a time only.

Fifth. — The hours of the club to be from 5 to 10, in the manner following: From 5 to 8 each member is at liberty to divert at cards, and in order to avoid the name of a gaming club, the following restriction shall be strictly observed viz: That no member shall presume or offer to play for more than twenty shillings at whist, picquet or any other game besides his club; on proof of gaming for any more, the member or members so offending shall pay the value of four bottles good wine for the use and benefit of the ensuing club night.

Sixth. — At eight of the clock the supper (if ready) to be brought in. At ten the club to be adjusted and paid, and no cards or any other game shall be allowed after supper.

Seventh.   — After supper if any of the members have any motion to make relating to the club he must wait till the chairman has just drank some loyal toast.

Eighth.   — That none of the members shall . . . during . . . conversation relating to Synagogue affairs, on the forfeit of the value of four bottles good wine for the use as aforesaid.

Ninth.   — If any of the members should behave unruly, curse, swear or offer fight, the chairman shall levy such fine as he sees fit, not exceeding, for each offence, four bottles good wine for the use aforesaid.

Tenth.   — If any of the members happen to be sick or absent, by acquainting Mr. Myer with the same, shall be exempt from paying anything towards the club, but if no notice given as aforesaid, shall pay his quota of the supper only.

Eleventh.   — If any of the members does not meet at club nights, and can't offer sufficient reason for so doing, the chairman with the members shall determine if he or they are to pay the proportion of the whole club, or the quota of supper only.

Twelfth.   — If any of the members neglect coming to club three nights successively without being sick or absent, shall be deemed unwilling, consequently his name shall be erased from the list, not to be admitted during the season without the consent of the chairman and all the members.

Thirteenth.— Every member after signing the articles, and not willing afterwards to conform to the same, his or their names shall be erased out of the list, and no more to be admitted during the season.

"In witness whereof the members of said club have signed their respective names the day and year above written.

Moses Lopez	Moses Levy
Isaac Polock	Isaacher Polock
Jacob Isaacs	Naph't Hart, Jr.
Abr'm Sarzedas	Jacob Rods, Rivera
Nap't Hart	

Fourteenth.—At a club held the 16th day of December, 1761, it is resolved and agreed by the chairman and the majority of all the members that these articles be inserted amongst the rules of said club, viz:

"That in case the chairman is not at the club, the secretary, for the time being, shall take his place, and the same obedience shall be paid him as if the chairman was present, and to be invested with equal authority. As also the said secretary is hereby empowered to nominate with the concurrence of the members then present, a secretary to supply his place for the time being; and that every month a secretary shall be elected in the same manner and form as the chairman is elected."

43. *PAJHS*, 19:4 ff.

2.

FREEDOM'S HOLY LIGHT

1. Edward Peterson, supra, p. 181.
2. *PAJHS* 2:105 ff.
3. Ibid. 21:15; Jewish Encyclopedia, vol. X, p. 432.
4. *PAJHS* 2:105 ff.
5. Jacob Rivera had a great reputation for honesty in business. It is told that business reverses and some losses at sea forced him into bankruptcy. When he recouped some of his losses and succeeded again in business he invited all of his creditors to a dinner, and placed under the plates a draft for the exact amount including the legal rate of interest due each creditor.
6. *PAJHS* 2:106.
7. Morris A. Gutstein, *Aaron Lopez and Judah Touro*, p. 17.
8. Ibid.
9. Quoted in Broches, supra, p. 62 ff.
10. Ibid. 61 ff
11. See letters in text, speaking about Religious objects and *Tephilin* that Mr. Abraham sent to the Lopez family.
12. Broches, supra, p. 64.
13. Ibid.
14. *PAJHS* 2:47.

3.

IN SERVICE OF GOD

1. *PAJHS* 29:35.
2. For this information I am indebted to Dr. David de Sola Pool of New York, who was gracious to have it copied for me from the archives in Amsterdam.

3. *PAJHS* 29:17, 24, 35; cf. Corcos, supra.
4. Ibid. 8:7, 189; 10:56, 157; 29:24; 44:219, 225, 228, 231.
5. Ibid. 29:16, 17.
6. Ibid. 10:46; 16:40.
7. Ibid. 28:23; 29:35.
8. Ibid. 6:78, 138; 13:93; 16:40; 29:17.
9. Pool, *Old Faith,* supra, 49, 169, 270 ff.
10. Harry Smith and J. Hugo Tatsch, *Moses Michael Hays,* p. 28 ff.
11. Ibid.
12. *Memoires of Samuel J. May,* p. 13 ff.
13. Stiles, op. cit. 1:379.
14. The children of Rev. Touro are usually given as three. Nathan was born in New York after Mr. Touro left Newport. He apparently died in childhood. See *PAJHS* 17:156.
15. Stiles, op. cit. p. 422.
16. Abiel Holmes, *The Life of Ezra Stiles,* p. 122 ff.

4.

A COLONIAL SANCTUARY

1. David de Sola Pool, *The Mill Street Synagogue of the Congregation Shearith Israel,* p. 3.
2. *PAJHS,* 27:407.
3. Esther I. Schwartz, *Touro Synagogue Restored, 1827-29,* in *Journal of the Society of Architectural Historians,* Summer, 1958, vol. 17, No. 2, p. 23 ff. I am indebted to Mr. J. D. Forbes, the editor of the Journal, for sending me the page-proofs of the article.
4. Ibid. p. 25 and note 10. The deed of the purchase of the land is dated June 13, 1759. In March of that year the Newport congregation addressed a letter to the New York congregation appealing for assistance to build the synagogue.
5. Book of Land Evidence of Newport, No. 14, pp. 412, 433, July 19, 1760.
   The ownership and the name of the Newport congregation present a problem, which played an important role at the end of the 19th century. At the time the land was purchased for the synagogue, in 1759, the congregation was not incorporated and could not purchase or own land. As a rule, some trusted individuals acting as trustees for the congregation purchased the land and held it in trust for the congregation. As a rule also, there was an agreement between these individuals and the congregation to the effect that the property belongs to the congregation, though the title to the land was

deeded to these individuals. (See D. de Sola Pool, *The Mill Street Synagogue*, etc. 22 ff. in reference to the deed and agreement between the *Congregation Shearith Israel* in New York and the trustees concerning the purchase of the land for the synagogue built in 1730. Also see PAJHS 27:181 in connection with the Newport synagogue, where the reference is found that Jacob R. Rivera, Moses Levy and Isaac Hart were also appointed as "trustees for building the synagogue.")

The record of the agreement between the Newport congregation and Rivera, Levy and Hart is not extant. However, J. R. Rivera in his will dated January 9, 1787, stated "I do hereby declare and make known unto all People that I have no exclusive right, title, of or to the Jewish Public Synagogue in Newport on account of the deed thereof, being made to myself, Moses Levy and Isaac Hart, which Isaac Hart thereafter conveyed his one part thereof to me, but that the same was done, meant and intended in trust only, to and for the sole use, benefit and behalf of the Jewish Society to be for them reserved as a place of Public Worship forever."

The title of the land was deeded to "Jacob Rodrigues Rivera, Moses Levy and Isaac Hart, their Heirs and Assigns forever." Inasmuch as Hart had assigned his share to Rivera, the legal title remained with Rivera and Levy. After the synagogue was closed for regular public worship because of the lack of a congregation (See chapter *Closed Are the Portals*) the last heirs of Rivera and Levy formally presented the title to the synagogue property (and the old cemetery which was taken to belong to the synagogue) to the *Congregation Shearith Israel* in New York. (See Pool, *An Old Faith in the New World*, p. 422). The legal ownership of the Newport synagogue by *Congregation Shearith Israel* was challenged several times, but it was finally established that the New York congregation is by right the legal owner of the Newport synagogue property, and therefore has the sole right to its disposition and management. (Pool, ibid.)

As to the name of the Newport congregation, it has generally been accepted that it was "Yeshuat Israel," and the synagogue is therefore referred to by all writers on the subject as the "Synagogue of Yeshuat Israel." (See Freedman and Gutstein, supra.) However nowhere in the early traceable records is the name "Yeshuat Israel" mentioned except in three places: on the title page of the Karigal sermon preached in 1773, on a document certifying the observance of the dietary laws, 1787 (See *Life Under Freedom*, infra), and on the monument dedicated to the memory of Reverend Isaac Touro in the old cemetery in Newport by his son Abraham in 1814.

(See Gutstein, p. 303). These references may be responsible for the fact that the name of the congregation was universally accepted to have been "Yeshuat Israel." However, in the correspondence of the Newport congregation and in the minutes of the *Congregation Shearith Israel* in New York extant, there is no reference to the actual name of the congregation in Newport. In *Three Centuries of Jewish Life in Curaçao* by Rabbi Is. Iessurun Cardozo, p. 47, the author states that at the time of the building of the synagogue in Newport the Congregation was called *Nephutsay Israel*. This is the first and only time that this reference was called to anyone's attention. It is based on a letter that the Newport congregation sent in 1765 to the *Congregation Mikvé Israel* in Willemstad, Curaçao, where before the signatures of the senders the name "K. K. Nepthusé Israel" appears.

Throughout the nineteenth century, the name of the congregation of the Newport Jewish community, at the time of the building of the synagogue, was accepted to have been *Congregation Yeshuat Israel*, which is the name ascribed to the congregation traditionally founded in 1658. In the letter that the Newport congregation addressed to the New York congregation in 1759 (See infra) asking for financial assistance in the building of the synagogue, the Newporters apologize for making this appeal on the basis that they are "a congregation yet in its infancy." This could hardly apply to a congregation which at the time of the writing of that letter was already 101 years old.

It is quite possible therefore that the Marranos and the new residents of the mid-eighteenth century organized a new congregation which they called for a time "Nephutsé Israel," which was subsequently supplanted by the original historic congregation that is said to have been founded in 1658, and called *Yeshuat Israel*.

To avoid misunderstandings, the author uses generally "Newport synagogue" or " "Newport congregation," until the middle of the nineteenth century when the synagogue began to be referred to generally as *Touro Synagogue*.

6. Book of Land Evidence, Vol. XV, p. 376.
    The value of the money according to the old tenor, as may be derived from a contemporary note by Stiles, was eight pounds for one dollar. Accordingly the purchasing price of the lot for the synagogue was $187.50, which was not such an enormous sum. Cf. The Literary Diary of Ezra Stiles, vol. 1, pp. 225-6.

7. Carl Bridenbaugh, *Peter Harrison, First American Architect*, p. 98, referring to *PAJHS*, 27: 181, 408.

8. *PAJHS*, 27: 177 ff.

9. Ibid. p. 179.
10. Ibid.
11. Ibid. p. 408 where the names of the congregations that helped the Newport synagogue are mentioned as part of the Yom Kippur Eve prayers. In that list Amsterdam is not mentioned.
12. Morris A. Gutstein, *A Newport Ledger,* 1760-1770, *PAJHS* 37:163.
13. Dedication Booklet of Congregation Jeshuat Israel Community Center, 1925
14. *PAJHS,* 27:181 ff.
15. Ibid.
16. Albert M. Hyamson, *The Sephardim of England,* p. 148-49.
17. Gutstein, p. 98 ff.
18. Ezra Stiles, supra, vol. 1, p. 6.
    Stiles copied the description of the dedication of the synagogue from the Newport Mercury, Dec. 5, 1763. This is obvious because the description appears in quotation marks in the diary.
19. A. Burnaby, *Travels Through the Middle Settlements in North America in the Year* 1759 *and* 1790, London 1775, p. 117 ff. See text infra, and note 31.
20. It may well be that the original color scheme was different. Some of the old residents in Newport informed me that they remembered some gold painting on the ceiling. Perhaps these were stars.
    As to the color that the bricks were painted outside, the yellowish tint might have been accidental and not to simulate the color of the ghetto walls.
21. Stiles, supra.
22. *The Ethics of the Fathers.* 4:17.
23. See text and notes 45-49 infra.
24. Esther I. Schwartz, supra, p. 26.
    While presumably there have been no fundamental changes in the interior of the synagogue since the dedication, except for painting and repair, Mrs. Esther I. Schwartz, in a recently published article "Touro Synagogue Restored, 1827-29" in the *Journal of the Society of Architectural Historians,* (supra) maintains that the present Ark and the Tablets of the Ten Commandments in the *Touro Synagogue* in Newport are different ones than the original ones. Mrs. Schwartz bases her conclusion on studies she made of some of the original documentary material associated with the *Touro Synagogue.* On the margin of the notes of the diary of the famous Dr. Ezra Stiles, which she examined in the manuscript collection of Yale University, Mrs. Schwartz found a sketch of the Ark drawn by the diarist at the time of the dedication of the synagogue, which though closet-like in appearance with four upright doors, and a framed

tablet of the Ten Commandments, appears to be different than the Ark of the historic synagogue today.

Since the synagogue was repaired in the interior and exterior between 1827 and 1829, Mrs. Schwartz comes to the conclusion, that it was during that period, specifically in 1828, sixty-five years after the dedication of the synagogue that a new Ark replaced the original. Mrs. Schwartz also suggests that the tablets of the Ten Commandments may have been painted at this time by one Ben. B. Howland, inasmuch as she found a bill of $12.00 by that gentleman for "Painting piece for Commandments." Since my knowledge of architectural designs is quite limited and my understanding of the architecture of the Touro Synagogue is based solely on the works of Bridenbaugh and Kimball, I do not want to assume the authoritative attitude and state categorically that Mrs. Schwartz is wrong. Nor, can I say equally that she is right. That in the course of time there might have been some repair or even slight changes in the woodwork of the enframement of the Decalogue and on the woodwork on the doors may be possible though not probable, as we can gather from what we do know of the *Touro Synagogue* in Newport.

However, the assumptions and conclusions of Mrs. Schwartz pose a number of important problems and significant questions. Why should anyone want to replace the old Ark with a new one in 1828, when there were no Jews in Newport at the time to use the synagogue or the Ark and it would serve no practical purpose?

No one doubts the fact that Peter Harrison was the architect of the Newport historic synagogue. All authorities agree that Harrison followed in all of his designs a certain definite pattern identified with the classical revival in eighteenth century architecture in England and in the colonies. Harrison's specific designs have been traced back to the plates and illustrations in the books of his extensive architectural library. All scholars agree that the Ark as we see it today is in perfect harmony with the general synagogue architecture, and reveals the colonial classical revival. The attic pediment and enframement certainly are in complete accord with the Greek columns and with the attic pediment of the portico. The woodwork and enframement of the Decalogue in Stiles' sketch is completely out of harmony with the rest of the architecture. If Stile's sketch represents the original Ark and not the one we have today, why should Harrison, who was so meticulous to details, have made an Ark not to fit the rest of the architecture in the building?

Then does "painting *piece for* (italics mine) commandments" mean painting a complete artistic oil canvas of the Ten Commandments with lettering and crowns and general flourishes that reveal the work of a master?

All repair in the synagogue in 1827-29 was done with the consent of the *Congregation Shearith Israel* in New York. Would not a major change like the replacement of the Ark and the painting of the Ten Commandments have been noted by the New York congregation and be reported in its minutes?

Finally, we might ask, are the differences in the rough drawing of Stiles' so marked from the present Ark, that we must assume that it was a different Ark that Stiles sketched? And if there were differences between the Ark and the rest of the architecture, would not Stiles have indicated it in his description?

While I do not presume to know all the answers, I would like to make a few observations in connection with these questions.

Let us consider first the painting of the Ten Commandments. There is no indication in Stiles' drawing of the traditional two columns indicating the two tablets with five commandments on each. Instead there is an incomplete Hebrew inscription of part of the second Commandment with a word outside of the tablet which obviously could not have been so originally.

That the inscription which Stiles gives could not be the complete inscription that appeared on the tablet and was made by the diarist simply as an illustration is obvious. For, the inscription as it appears in Stiles' sketch translates: "Thou shalt have no god." Such an inscription on an Ark is hardly conceivable. Besides the commandments on a synagogue Ark would certainly begin with what in Jewish tradition is the first commandment "I am the Eternal Thy God who brought Thee out of the land of Egypt, out of the house of bondage," or with the first words thereof.

In addition to this: "piece for commandments" does not mean commandments. It may well refer to the painting of the frame, the woodwork and the other embellishment around the tablet of the commandments, which Mr. Howland painted. Then, we must not forget the crowns above the Ten Commandments in the present painting, which indicate not only Rabbinic knowledge but requires interpretation. There can be no doubt that whoever designed the tablets of the commandments with the crowns, had some fundamental knowledge of Rabbinic literature or was guided by someone who possessed that knowledge. The idea of the three crowns is based on the *Ethics of the Fathers,* the Rabbinic treatise in which the reference is found. This idea could not have been executed without the presence of some Jews in Newport who were acquainted with *The Ethic of the Fathers.* There were no Jews in Newport during the repairing of the Touro Synagogue in 1827-1829; and there is no reference found that the New York *Congregation Shearith Israel,* that already owned the synagogue during that time, and with whose consent the repairs were undertaken by the Municipal authorities, sent anyone to Newport to supervise the painting or to suggest the painting of the crowns.

In addition to this it has been pointed out by experts that the canvas-painting of the Decalogue in the *Touro Synagogue* in Newport reveals the hand of a skillful artist. Certainly an artist of that type even were he an amateur, would have painted other things, and would be known in some manner. A search in all reference works to American artists in the library of the Art Institute in Chicago did not reveal the name of Ben Howland.

It is probable therefore that "painting piece for Commandments," more logically refers to woodwork around the canvas painting, rather than to the painting of the Ten Commandments proper.

As to the Ark, it may be well to note that Stiles' description of it, in his account of the dedication, and the description of the interior during the dedication, fits much more the present Ark than the scketch in his notes. Then the Ark with the four upright doors, the woodwork and all the embellishments also match closely all other architectural features in the interior.

Bridenbaugh, Kimball, Hitchcock and others have succeeded in tracing the designs of the Ark to the plates that were used by Harrison in other buildings. (See figures 33-35 in Bridenbaugh *Peter Harrison*). In addition to this, a year before the dedication, in 1762, Moses Lopez, the president of the Newport congregation in writing to New York mentions the fact that workingmen were engaged to finish the Hechal (Ark) by Rosh Hashanah. (See *PAJHS* 27:179). This would of necessity mean that Harrison had supervision over its construction. Certainly it would not be logical to assume that the Ark was not in consonance with the rest of the architectural designs and needed to be replaced six or seven decades later.

We may also assume, until we find out otherwise, that Stiles may very well have sketched the Ark in his notes in contrast with the one he observed in the Newport synagogue. He might have sketched from memory the Ark of the New York synagogue which he saw in 1754 (See Pool *Old Faith, etc.*). For it stands to reason Stiles did not draw the sketch of the Ark until he returned home from the synagogue dedication. (It is not conceivable that he carried along his diary with him to record events.) It is also possible that he did it a few days later, because it seems that his description of the dedication, Stiles copied from the Newport Mercury which appeared three days after the dedication. The quotation marks in the description of the dedication by Stiles would indicate that it was copied from another source. Thus Stiles' sketch of the Ark may be either a faulty sketch of the Newport Ark or a possible sketch of the New York Ark.

25. Structure-wise twelve columns were not needed except to have some symbolic meaning. For, a lesser number of columns would conceivably have been enough. Knowing that columns are generally expensive and that the Newport congregation was considerably short in funds many times, were it not symbolic, less than twelve columns would have surely satisfied the congregation. See also text, infra, where it is pointed out that the Amsterdam and London synagogues had twelve columns.

26. The Perpetual Light bears the inscription "The Gift of Samuel Judah of New York." The large candelabrum bears the inscription "the Gift of Jacob Pollack."

27. Two of the smaller candelabra are inscribed "the Gift of Abraham Rodrigues Rivera," one "the Gift of Naphtali Hart Myers," and one "the Gift of Aaron Lopez."

     The candlesticks were donated by Enoch Lyons.

28. Dr. Pool informed me that to build a secret passage did not seem a universal custom in the Sephardic synagogues built either during or after the Inquisition. However, since the principal builders of the Touro Synagogue were former Marranos, the situation here might have been different. However, see text and note 51, infra.

29. That there was a *Mikveh* is definite. Dr. Stiles refers to a public ritual bath called "Bagnio" which was attended by "More strict Jews" who "baptize religiously by trine Immersion three times a year, at Passover, and I think Pentecost and Day of Atonement; that is, it is a religious Purification with them." See *The Literary Diary of Ezra Stiles*, vol. 1, p. 256, where the *Mikveh* is described as a bath "where there are Stairs to the Bottom where one stands to his neck in water."

30. Bridenbaugh, supra p. 120.

31. Quoted in Ibid, p. 110 from Burnaby, op. cit.

32. Fiske Kimball, *Peter Harrison* in *Touro Synagogue of Congregation Jeshuat Israel*, published on the occasion of the dedication of the synagogue as a *National Historic Site*, p. 14 ff. See also Appendices in Bridenbaugh, on the collection of books by Peter Harrison.

33. Another painting of the Ten Commandments with old Spanish underneath each commandment and the imaginary likeness of Moses and Aaron on each side was hung in another part of the edifice.

See Hyamson, *Sephardim*, etc., op. cit.

34. Kimball, supra.
35. Cf. Lee M. Friedman, *Pilgrims in a New Land*, p. 132 and note 5.
36. Rachel Wishnitzer, *Synagogue Architecture in the United States*, p. 15 ff.
37. Pool, *Old Faith, etc.* supra, p. 44 ff.
38. Wishnitzer, supra 3 ff.
39. Ibid.
40. An engraving of the Amsterdam synagogue as well as ground plans of the building were made in 1675. These might well have been available to Harrison or to some of the Jewish residents in Newport who came from Amsterdam. See Wishnitzer, supra.
41. Bridenbaugh, supra, p. 99.
42. See text infra and note 45.
43. Friedman, supra.
44. Kimball, supra; Bridenbaugh, supra.
45. Ibid.
46. See Appendices in Bridenbaugh, supra.
47. Wischnitzer, supra, p. 16.
48. See figures 33-35 in Bridenbaugh.
49. Wischnitzer, supra.
50. Bridenbaugh, supra.
51. A. F. Downing and V. J. Scully, Jr., *The Architectural Heritage of Newport, Rhode Island*, p. 80; E. F. Robinson and T. P. Robinson, *Houses in America*.
52. Genesis. 28:17

5.

LIFE UNDER FREEDOM

1. *Shearith Israel Minutes*, March 5, 1775. See Pool, *Old Faith, etc.*, p. 422. The size of the Jewish community of Newport in the eighteenth century has been grossly exaggerated by its admirers. In spite of the continuous influx of Jews into Newport which had begun at the end of the seventeenth century, the population of the city by the middle of the eighteenth century and later, on the eve of the American Revolution, remained comparatively small. According to some, a ship that sailed from Portugal to Virginia carrying a contingent of Marranos who escaped from their native land after the earthquake in Lisbon, sought refuge in Narragansett Bay from bad winds and its passengers settled in Newport in 1755. Others claim that Aaron Lopez wrote to Jeremiah Osborne who was

in charge of a ship going from London to Lisbon and then back to
the colonies, "Should any of my friends in Lisbon incline to come
with you, I need not recommend you to use them with the same
tenderness that I might expect myself from you." This was taken
as evidence that Lopez induced forty Jewish families to settle in
Newport. All are unanimous that by the time of the dedication
of the synagogue there were from sixty to seventy Jewish families
in the city. A decade later, some claim Newport harbored 1175
Jews of the 2000 in all the colonies, and that there were 300
worshippers at the synagogue at this time. Yet, an observer of the
dedication noted: "There may be Eighty Souls of Jews or 15
families now in town." This number seems to have been the same
in 1765. The increase was gradual and slow. In 1764 Stiles wrote
to London: "We have 15 or 20 Families of Jews here, almost
the only ones in New England." In 1769 he noted. "There are
now in Town about Twenty-five Families of Jews." And in 1770,
in recording the various religious societies in Newport, Stiles gives
the Jewish population as consisting of 30 families. Another contemporary in 1771 recorded the "number of Jews of all ages and
sexes 121." According to the official census taken by the order
of the General Assembly on June 1, 1774, there appear to have
been at that time in Newport about twenty-five families that can
be identified as Jewish, a total number of 158 people. Of these
46 were males over 16 years of age, 21 males under 16, 52 female
persons over 16, and 39 under 16. This census, however, is not
all inclusive. A number of Jewish people did not desire to submit
to counting due to religious reasons. Hence, a number of Jewish
families, who lived in Newport at the time, are omitted. We may
note especially the Rivera family.

2. The centrality of the synagogue in Jewish community life and
    activities was universal in that period. See chapter "Centrality of the
    Synagogue" in Pool's *An Old Faith in the New World*, p. 233 ff.
3. Stiles op. cit. 1:374. Stiles notes how Rabbi Karigal corrected the
    reading of the Reverend Isaac Touro of the word in Leviticus 25:29,
    which is to be pronounced "gaulto" a Sephardic pronunciation of
    the word.
4. *PAJHS* 27:453.
5. Stiles, op. cit, p. 378 ff. pp. 293, 377, 403.
6. Gutstein, text and notes 35-40 in chapter *A Glimpse at Jewish
    Life* pp. 177 ff., 358.
7. Ibid.
8. Copied from one of the Shipping Books in the Newport Historical
    Society archives.

9. An examination of the Shipping Book of Aaron Lopez reveals this.
10. Washburn, *History of Leicester, Mass.*, p. 122f.
11. See Bibliography for full title of book.
12. Channing, pp. 199-202.
13. Ibid.
14. Ibid.
15. Stiles, op. cit. p. 256.
16. *PAJHS* 2:104 ff.; *Commerce of Rhode Island* 1:196.
17. *Diary of Frederick MacKinzie,* quoted in *Newport Historical Society Bulletin,* No. 93, p. 8.
18. *Johann Doehla Tagebuch,* (in German ms.) in New York Public Library, translated by Erich A. O'D. Taylor.
19. Stiles, op. cit. vol. 1, p. 19. The Messianic calculations were based on the text in Daniel 7:25, where in the interpretation by Daniel of the dream of Belshazzar, in which he saw four great beasts come up from the sea the words *idan, idanin, uplag idan,* occur. This is interpreted as *time times and a half,* in accordance with the text quoted by Stiles. In New York, the Messiah was expected in 1768. See Pool, *Old Faith, etc.*
20. Stiles, op. cit. p. 32.
21. Ibid, p. 377.
21a. Stiles op. cit. 1:403.
22. There were congregations in New York, Philadelphia, Savannah, Georgia and Charleston, South Carolina. The congregation in New York had its own synagogue built and dedicated in 1730. This was really the first synagogue in North America. Another congregation was founded later in Richmond, Va. In 1790 that Congregation joined the others in sending an address to George Washington.
22a. Stiles op. cit. p. 392.
23. Under July 5, 1783, Stiles summarized the visits of these rabbis to Newport.
23a. Shipping Book of Aaron Lopez, 1771-73; Letter of 1767 in Newport Historical Society vaults; *PAJHS* 27:185.
24. *PAJHS* 27:185. See original letters in Newport Historical Society and American Jewish Historical Society (New York) vaults. See also Edwin Wolf II and Maxwell Whiteman, *The History of the Jews of Philadelphia,* p. 56.
25. The author read a paper "A Chassidic Rabbi Visits Newport," based on one such letter, before one of the Annual Meetings of the A.J.H.S. Some Yiddish letters have been published in *PAJHS*.
26. From the sermon by Rabbi Karigal.

6.

TO BIGOTRY NO SANCTION

1. Charles Caroll, *Rhode Island, Three Centuries of Democracy,* vol. 1, p. 264; *Commerce of Rhode Island,* op. cit.
2. *Stiles,* op. cit. vol. 1, p. 448.
3. Ibid, p. 29.
4. *PAJHS,* 27:156.
5. The date of demise is usually given as Dec. 8, 1783. However, the Hebrew date on the monument, Tebet 14, corresponds to Jan. 8, 1784 and not Dec. 8, 1783.
6. *Newport Historical Bulletin* No. 6, p. 9.
7. See chapter 10 infra.
8. The texts of the letters were copied from the facsimilies in Gutstein, p. 210 ff.

7.

CLOSED ARE THE PORTALS

1. Gutstein, p. 225; *PAJHS* 27:424.
2. Ibid.
3. Pool, *Old Faith* op. cit. p. 421 ff.
4. Ibid.
5. Ibid.
6. See correspondence between Moses Lopez and Nathan H. Gould in *PAJHS* 27:423 ff.
7. George G. Channing, *Early Recollections of Newport.*
8. Quoted in *Journal of the Society of Architectural Historians,* vol. 17, no. 2, p. 23.
9. This date is a mystery. It should be 1658, unless the author refers to the contingent of Jews who came to Newport in the '90s of the 17th century from Curaçao.
10. The Will was copied in the Municipal Records of the City of Newport.
11. See Appendix K in Gutstein, p. 329 ff.
12. Ibid.
13. See Note 6 supra.
14. Ibid.
15. *Journal of the Society of Architectural Historians,* op. cit.

8.

THE SACRED SHRINE IS HOLY YET

1. *Rhode Island American and General Advertiser,* vol. 14, June 14, 1822, quoted in *Journal* ibid.
2. A paper on the contents of these scrap-books by Dr. Pool was published under the title *The Touro Synagogue: Aspects of the Missing Half-Century of Its History,* in *PAJHS* 38:57-76.
3. See *Gutstein,* p. 256 ff.
4. Ibid.
5. See note 5 on Chapter 4, in refernce to name of congregation.
6. *Minutes of Board of Trustees* of the Congregation Shearith Israel, New York (ms.) vol. 7, pp. 200, 202; Pool, *The Mill Street Synagogue,* p. 49 ff.
7. Extracts of Will of Judah Touro and other agreements in Appendices in Gutstein. See also ibid. p. 258.
8. Pool, *Old Faiths,* etc., p. 423 ff.
9. Ibid.
10. Gutstein, p. 260; Minutes of Congregation Shearith Israel, vol. 7, p. 204.
11. Ibid
12. Hyamson, *The History of the Sephardim,* op. cit.
13. Newport Mercury, June 2, 1883. I am indebted to Mr. H. O. Brigham of the Newport Historical Society and to the Hon. Erich A. O'D. Taylor of Newport for sending me this quotation.
14. See note 2.
15. For a detailed discussion on the controversies between the respective congregations in Newport and their attempts to possess the Touro Synagogue, and between these congregations and the *Congregation Shearith Israel* in New York, see David C. Adelman, *They Broke In To Pray* in *Rhode Island Jewish Historical Notes,* Vol. 2, No. 4, April 1958, pp. 226-237.
16. Pool, *Old Faith,* etc., supra, p. 424.
17. Minutes of the Board of Trustees of the *Congregation Shearith Israel,* vol. 7, p. 46.
18. See about name of old congregation note 5, chapter 4. The old spelling was "Yeshuat." The new spelling was the Germanized "Jeshuat."
19. See minutes, *Shearith Israel,* Jan. 9, April 10, May 31, July 2, Oct. 14, 29, Nov. 19, 1900; Pool, *Old Faith, etc.* supra, pp. 425, 531.
20. Gutstein, p. 271 ff., and note 4.

21. Constitution, By-Laws and Rules of the *K. K. Jeshuat Israel*, 1894, pp. 11, 1, 13.
22. Historical Background and By-Laws of the Congregation Jeshuat Israel of Newport, R. I. Adopted January 28, 1945, p. 17.
23. State of Rhode Island Acts and Resolves 1899. The members of the "Touro Congregation" broke in to the synagogue to pray and to forcibly take possession of the synagogue. Some were arrested and brought to trial. The claim of the "Touro Congregation" to the possession and use of the Touro Synagogue and the Touro funds that were left for the Touro synagogue was based on Rivera's will where he stated that he held the title of the Newport synagogue "in trust only to and for the sole use, benefit and behalf of the Jewish Society." The "Touro Congregation" now considered itself the "Jewish Society" of Newport with the rights to the synagogue. The court did not uphold this contention. See Adelman, supra note 15.
24. Pool *Old Faith,* supra, p. 424 ff.
25. Adelman, op. cit. (note 15); Newport Daily News, March 31, 1899; July 11, 1899.
26. Ibid. Also see Gutstein, p. 276.
27. Pool, *Old Faith, etc.,* p. 425.
28. Ibid.
29. Gutstein, p. 275 ff.
30. Information received from Rabbi Seidel, of blessed memory.
31. Minutes of Board of Trustes of *Congregation Shearith Israel.*

9.

AND REMEMBERED BE FOR GOOD

1. The year should be 5643-1883. On both tablets there are Hebrew inscriptions of Biblical verses.
2. The address by Mr. Huhner was published under the title *The Jews of Newport* in a separate pamphlet. A copy of this pamphlet is found in the Newport Historical Society.
3. *Newport Herald* and *Newport Daily News,* Sept. 8, 1908.
4. Manual of Congregation Jeshuat Israel published in 1945, p. 52.
5. Newport Herald, May 27, 1933.
6. Newport Daily News, May 27, 1933.
7. The radio address was printed in the Newport Herald, May 30, 1933.
8. Newport Herald, May 29, 1933.
9. Newport Daily News, May 29, 1933.

10. Anniversary Program Book.
11. The proclamation appears in a special brochure published, for Jewish Day.
12. Ibid.
13. Newport Herald, July 6, 1936.
14. There was no formal presentation of the book. This volume is now out of print. The subtitle of the book is *Two and a Half Centuries of Judaism*, 1658-1908, published by Bloch Publishing Co., New York.
15. From Introduction to book.
16. Letter of Dr. Luce in author's files.

10.

A MONUMENT TO LIBERTY AND A NATIONAL SHRINE

1. Invitation to Service.
2. Newport Daily News, June 24, 1939. Newport Herald, June 24, 1939.
3. Ibid.
4. Ibid.
5. Ibid.
6. Ibid.
7. Ibid.
8. Invitation to Exercises.
9. The exact date when religious and civil liberty was formally declared in Rhode Island cannot be ascertained. The fact is that religious liberty was practiced in Providence since its founding in 1636 and in Newport since 1639. However, the charter granted the colony in 1663 expressly formulated the doctrine of religious liberty.

   The selection for the inscription was a subject of long discussion. This inscription was suggested by the author and approved by Dr. Pool.
10. Newport Herald and Newport Daily News, August 21, 1939.
11. Ibid.
12. Ibid.
13. Ibid.
14. The title of the book is *Aaron Lopez and Judah Touro - A Refugee and the Son of a Refugee.*
15. The presentation of the book was part of the general Tercentenary observance and the invitations carried the official seal of the City Tercentenary Committee.

16. Newport Herald and Newport Daily News, Nov. 1, 1939.
17. Ibid.
18. Ibid.
19. Some of the Yiddish and Anglo-Jewish press carried news items of the event.
20. From original script of program.
21. The address was published as a brochure and also in several newspapers under the title *Equality versus Toleration*. In 1952, the author received the Freedom's Foundation medal and award for this sermon.
22. Newport News, August 19, 1940.
23. Professor Bridenbaugh subsequently (1945) published it in his book *Peter Harrison, First American Architect*. This quotation is from the book, p. 100 ff.
24. Newport Herald, Aug. 19, 1940.
25. The major contents of the address of Dr. Pool was published in a brochure "George Washington and Religious Liberty." These quotations are taken from this brochure.
26. Thomas J. Allen, *Touro Synagogue as a National Historical Site*, in *Touro Synagogue of Congregation Jeshuat Israel, Newport, Rhode Island*, supra, p. 51.
27. Copied from agreement sent to the author by Dr. Pool.
28. See *PAJHS* 38:57.
29. Newport Daily News, Sept. 1-2, 1947. I am indebted to Mr. Herbert O. Brigham, Librarian of the Newport Historical Society and to Hon. Erich A. O'D. Taylor for sending me copies of the newspaper's report of the dedicatory exercises.
30. This was only temporary and for a few summers only.
31. The phrase "To bigotry no sanction, to persecution no assistance" was first used by Moses Seixas in his address to the president on behalf of the *Hebrew Congregation of Newport*. George Washington merely repeated it in his address.
32. From poem "America" by Edgar A. Guest.

APPENDIX

1. Mrs. Esther I. Schwartz in her paper on the restoration of the Touro Synagogue (typewritten copy loaned to author by Mrs. Schwartz) called attention to the fact that, "In 1823 we found listed in the Sessions Laws of the State of Rhode Island *Acts and Resolves to secure and appropriate the Touro Jewish Synagogue.*"
2. Minutes of the Town Council of Newport. I am indebted to Mr.

Herbert O. Brigham of the Newport Historical Society, where the minute books are deposited, for this reference and quotation.

3. Morris A. Gutstein, *Aaron Lopez and Judah Touro,* p. 101.
4. Leon Huhner, *The Life of Judah Touro,* 1775-1854, p. 118, ff.
5. Ibid.
6. I. J. Benjamin, *Three Years in America,* vol. 2, p. 320 ff.
7. Ibid.
8. Benjamin suggested that due to the greater problems caused by the Civil War the Touro Monument project was abandoned.

SELECTED BIBLIOGRAPHY

American Jewish Year Book, 1900-1.

Arnold, Samuel Green, *History of the State of Rhode Island,* Providence, R. I., 1894.

Bartlett, John Russell (editor), *Colonial Records of Rhode Island and Providence Plantations,* Providence, 1856.
— *Census of the Inhabitants of the Colony of Rhode Island and Providence Plantations 1774,* Providence, 1858.

Bicknell, Thomas William, *History of Rhode Island and Providence Plantations,* New York, 1920.

Bigelow, Bruce M., *Aaron Lopez, Merchant of Newport* in the *New England Quarterly,* Vol. IV, No. 4, October 1931.

Bridenbaugh, Carl, *Peter Harrison, First American Architect,* Chapel Hill, 1949.

Broches, S. *Jews in New England,* N. Y. 1942.

Cardozo, I. Jessurun (editor), *Oldest Synagogue in the New World — Three Centuries of Jewish Life in Curaçao, 1654-1954,* Curaçao, 1955

Carroll, Charles, *Rhode Island, Three Centuries of Democracy,* New York, 1932.

Channing, George G., *Early Recollections of Newport,* Newport, 1868.

City Documents of Newport, R. I., Published by the City.

City Documents of Newport, Rhode Island, In manuscript in the office of the Clerk of the City of Newport, City Hall.

Cohen, George, *Jews in the Making of America,* Boston, 1924.

Commerce of Rhode Island: Published by, and as part of, Massachusetts Historical Society, Seventh Series, 1914-15.

Corcos, Joseph M., *A Synopsis of the History of the Jews of Curaçao,* Curaçao, 1897.

Daly, Charles P., *The Settlement of the Jews in North America* (Edited with notes by Max J. Kohler), New York 1893.

Dexter, F. B., *Literary Diary of Ezra Stiles,* New York, 1901.

Downing, A. F. and Scully, Jos. V. J., *The Architectural Heritage of*

Newport, Rhode Island, 1640-1915, Cambridge, 1952.
Files of
Newport Daily News
Newport Mercury
Newport Herald
Friedman, Lee M., *Early American Jews*, Cambridge, 1934.
— *The Newport Synagogue* in *Old-Time New England*, Vol. 36, Jan. 1946.
— *Pilgrims in a New Land*, Philadelphia, 1948.
Goodman, Abram V., *American Overture - Jewish Rights in Colonial Times*. Philadelphia, 1947.
Grinstein, Hyman B., *The Rise of the Jewish Community of New York, 1654-1860*, Philadelphia, 1945.
Gutstein, Morris A., *The Story of the Jews of Newport, Two and a Half Centuries of Judaism, 1658-1908*, New York 1936.
— *The Touro Family in Newport*. Newport, 1935.
— *A Newport Ledger 1760-1770*, in *PAJHS* 37:163.
—*Aaron Lopez and Judah Touro*. New York, 1939.
Handlin, Oscar, *Adventure in Freedom*, New York, 1954.
Heads of Families at the First Census of the United States, Taken in the Year 1790, Rhode Island (reprint), Washington, 1908.
Huhner, Leon, *The Life of Judah Touro*, Philadelphia, 1946.
Hyamson, Albert M., *The Sephardim of England*, London, 1951.
Janowsky, Oscar, *The American Jew*, New York, 1942.
Jastrow, M., *References to Jews in the Diary of Ezra Stiles*, in *PAJHS* vol. 10
Kimball, Fiske, *The Colonial Amateurs and Their Models* in *Architecture*, Vols. 53-54, June-July 1926.
Kohler, Max J., *Jews in Newport*, in *PAJHS* 6:61 - 80.
Kohut, George Alexander, *Ezra Stiles and the Jews*. New York, 1922.
Lebeson, Anita Libman, *Pilgrim People*. New York, 1950.
Lopez Correspondence and Business Books, in manuscript, found in the vaults of the Newport Historical Society.
Marcus, Jacob R., *Early American Jewry*, Vol. 1, Philadelphia, 1951.
Markens, Isaac, *The Hebrews in America*, New York, 1888.
Mason, George C., *Reminiscences of Newport*, Newport, 1884.
Masserman, Paul and Baker, Max, *Jews Come to America*, New York, 1943.
Mendes, Abraham Pereira, *The Jewish Cemetery at Newport*, in *Rhode Island Historical Magazine*, Vol. 6, October 1885.
Newport Historical Society Bulletins, published by the Society since January 1912.

Newport and Rhode Island Historical Magazine, published by the New-
port Historical Society. First number appeared in 1880.
Oppenheim, Samuel, *The First Settlement of the Jews in Newport,
Some New Matter on the Subject,* in *PAJHS* 34:7.
—— *The Jews and Masonry in the United States before 1810*
in *PAJHS* 19:11.
Peterson, Edward, *History of Rhode Island and Newport.* New York,
1853.
Pool, David de Sola and Tamar, *An Old Faith in the New World,
Portrait of Shearith Israel 1654-1954,* New York, 1955.
Pool, David de Sola, *Portraits Etched in Stone,* New York, 1952.
—— *The Touro Synagogue, Aspects of the Missing Half-Century of
Its History, 1850-1900,* in *PAJHS* 38:57.
Publications of the American Jewish Historical Society, Published by the
Society since 1893.
Ross, Arthur A., *A Discourse Embracing the Civil and Religious History
of Rhode Island.* Providence, 1838.
Samuel, Wilfred S., *A Review of the Jewish Colonists in Barbados in
the year 1688,* London, 1936.
Schappes, Morris U., *A Documentary History of the Jews in the United
States 1654-1875.* New York, 1950.
Schwartz, Esther I., *Touro Synagogue Restored, 1827-29,* in *Journal of
the Society of Architectural Historians,* vol. XVII, No. 2.
Strauss, Oscar, *Roger Williams,* New York, 1899.
Touro Synagogue Publications,
    *Brochure on 50th Anniversary of the Reconsecration of the Syna-
    gogue 1883-1933.*
    Rhode Island Tercentenary 1636-1936. Jewish Day, July 5, 1936.
    *Touro Synagogue of Congregation Jeshuat Israel, Newport, Rhode
    Island Founded 1658,* Published on occasion of Dedication of
    Synagogue as Nationl Shrine, Newport, 1948.
    *The Congregation Jeshuat Israel of Newport, Rhode Island, Manual,
    Historical Background and By-Laws,* Newport 1945.
    *The Old Jewish Community of Newport, Rhode Island with Sketch
    of the Ancient Touro Synagogue and Cemetery.* Newport, 1905.
Washburn, Emory, *History of Leicester, Mass.,* Boston, 1860.
Weeden, William B. *Early Rhode Island,* New York, 1910.
Wiernik, Peter, *The History of the Jews in America,* New York, 1932.
Wischnitzer, Rachel, *Synagogue Architecture in the United States,*
Philadelphia, 1955.
Wolf, Simon, *The American Jew as Patriot, Soldier and Citizen,*
New York, 1895.

INDEX

189